Intellectual Properties and the Protection of Fictional Characters

INTELLECTUAL PROPERTIES AND THE PROTECTION OF FICTIONAL CHARACTERS

Copyright, Trademark, or Unfair Competition?

Dorothy J. Howell

Q

QUORUM BOOKS

New York • Westport, Connecticut • London

Library of Congress Cataloging-in-Publication Data

Howell, Dorothy J.
Intellectual properties and the protection of fictional characters : copyright, trademark, or unfair competition? / Dorothy J. Howell.
p. cm.
Includes bibliographical references.
ISBN 0–89930–506–7 (lib. bdg. : alk. paper)
1. Copyright—Motion pictures—United States. 2. Copyright—Caricatures and cartoons—United States. 3. Trademarks—United States. 4. Competition, Unfair—United States. I. Title.
KF3050.H69 1990
346.7304'8—dc20
[347.30648] 89–49434

British Library Cataloguing in Publication Data is available.

Library of Congress Catalog Card Number: 89–49434
ISBN: 0–89930–506–7

First published in 1990

Quorum Books, 88 Post Road West, Westport, CT 06881
An imprint of Greenwood Publishing Group, Inc.

The paper used in this book complies with the Permanent Paper Standard issued by the National Information Standards Organization (Z39.48–1984).

10 9 8 7 6 5 4 3 2 1

For Avice and Clifford
With the deepest gratitude and fond memories

Contents

Preface

Is a fictional character legally recognized as intellectual property and thus protected by either copyright or trademark or else by principles of unfair competition? The very popularity of latter-day fictional heroes renders them vulnerable to appropriation, innocent as well as illicit. Such heroes represent valuable properties in the entertainment marketplace, and the courts frequently are called on to protect them. It has been said that protection of these properties is either nonexistent or inadequate.

The question and a negative response to it are not only of concern to the legal community. Those who create or promote fictional characters for all the media of popular culture need a pragmatic understanding of how and to what extent their creations can be legally protected. Authors and other artists need to know the limitations of legal protection, along with the more subtle pitfalls for the unwary. Only then will they understand the essential ingredients of effective licensing agreements. Only then is the artist who is inspired to build on another's creation apprised of the subtle borderline separating legitimate development from an illicit taking.

In this book, through a selection of cases chosen for their bearing on the popular arts, basic principles are reviewed as a preliminary to intensive analysis of their application to fictional characters in search of legal protection. The foremost protection is found in the federal Copyright Act, complemented by the Lanham Act regulating trademarks. While these codifications of the constitutional exhortation to promote the progress of useful arts go far in establishing—and limiting—legal protection, the case law, governed in large measure by equitable principles, will be the ultimate determinant of any rights, duties, or liabilities associated with a fictional character. Although intellectual properties may be intangible, standard principles of procedure and substance flowing from the Constitution, statutes, and the judiciary are invoked in their recognition and ultimate distribution.

Superimposed on statutory provisions is case law in contract and, more often, in tort. Legitimate distribution of copyright and trademark properties is accomplished through licensing agreements. Illicit takings are subject to tort sanctions. Hence the law of intellectual property is an integral part of the American legal system. It is also a crucial component in the American marketplace.

The intellectual property known as copyright, subject to the preemptive federal Copyright Act, requires the original and unique expression of an idea. For a finite interval of time the author of that expression enjoys the exclusive right to reproduce it in a variety of media. Because outright copying—direct plagiarism—is rare, the judicial inference of a taking is most often supported by proof of the defendant's access to the plaintiff's work, accompanied by substantial similarity in the expression of the two works.

While comparison of ideas pursuant to an objective "extrinsic" analysis is straightforward and relatively simple, a comparison of expression through the subjective "intrinsic" approach can be complex and quite subtle. The latter may actually demand the sensitivity to the medium of expression usually expected of respected critics.

Once the basic elements of copyright infringement are set forth, the court examines applications through case law. Ordinarily, the court will begin with a comparison of the ideas conveyed by competing works. Then, if they are found to be similar, the court compares form of expression, incorporating questions of law and fact. Today's transformations across media and the current merchandising phenomenon, carrying characters and other elements of the popular arts well beyond their media of origin, add multiple layers of complexity to judicial review. In the end, judicially imposed distributions can depend on the highly subjective matters of total *concept* and *feel* conveyed by competing expressions. The court may apply objective and subjective tests in the effort to resolve the frequently close question of substantial similarity, but it will look at the competing works as a reader or viewer would, not as either of the creators does.

Copyright cases reveal a continuum ranging from a bare idea to full-fledged expression. It is no surprise that the subject of reported cases almost always falls near the center of the continuum, with the court struggling to place it with sufficient accuracy to resolve the infringement issue and impose appropriate sanctions where a taking is found.

In addition to reviewing the illustrative cases through which copyright elements and defenses to infringement are presented, this book reviews the litigation surrounding the film *Star Wars* and its lesser competitor, *Battlestar Galactica*, in some detail. Characters and characterization represent a crucial component in judicial efforts to resolve this controversy.

The intellectual property known as trademark is something of a companion to that champion of protection known as copyright. Trademark in this context is frequently attended by the more nebulous unfair competition. Trademark can attach to the intellectual properties of interest here. Certain titles and many characters, along with elements from their fictional worlds, can assume the status of a trademark.

Since trademark specifically protects name and, sometimes, physical appearance, it can extend the scope of protection afforded fictional characters. Not only can resultant protection extend beyond the limits of copyright, but trademark also holds the potential for indefinite protection.

Trademark, like copyright, is subject to actionable infringement. Unlike copyright, however, trademark depends heavily upon the consuming public, first for continued existence of the property and then for the determination of a misappropriation. Unlike copyright, a trademark risks being abandoned and rendered generic. Moreover, trademark can be usurped by public usage and enter the public domain (i.e., "become generic") notwithstanding the best efforts of its proprietor.

Trademark protects the source of a product, including a fictional character and his world, from three kinds of taking: confusion of the public; passing off (or palming off) of another's product as that of the source; and dilution, a less direct reduction in the mark's value as an indicator of source. Trademark is of particular interest here because three contemporary heroic figures of extraordinary popularity are in fact trademarks. They are the Lone Ranger, Superman, and Tarzan of the Apes.

The integration of copyright, trademark, unfair competition principles, and contract law in the protection of fictional characters is revealed through analyses of trends in the relevant case law, especially that of the Second Circuit (New York City) and Ninth Circuit (California), which represent two renowned centers of the arts and hear most of the cases arising from the popular literary and dramatic arts. Of special interest is the Sam Spade case in which the Ninth Circuit held a character to be uncopyrightable yet retained—as an unnamed intellectual property—by the creating author for future use in new works. Case law in this circuit is compared with that in the Second Circuit, where copyright in character is expressly recognized.

The Lone Ranger and Superman are examples of successful legal protection as well as its undeniable limitations. The legal fate of the prototype for television's popular Paladin provides contrast. More of the limitations in protection are revealed through the unsuccessful legal campaign of the original Paladin's author. The saga constitutes a vivid warning for any who would "sleep on their rights" or who have little financial stake in a character.

Yet another approach—and an extraordinarily successful one—is demonstrated through the artful combination of retention, licensing, and accommodation of the public fascination surrounding *Star Trek*. The Enterprise's ensemble of provocative characters, especially Mr. Spock, own a special place not only in today's popular culture but also in successful legal management—apparently with little resort to litigation.

All the theories and principles of legal protection are integrated in the phenomenal creation, delineation, distribution, and litigation surrounding Edgar Rice Burroughs's Tarzan of the Apes. Approaching classic status, the literary Tarzan arises from rich cultural sources, yet is unique. Despite his unique character, Tarzan has been absorbed into popular culture as no other genre-hero has before or since. And yet Tarzan is quite obviously at least two different persona in competition, each of whom is separately and fully protected by an assortment of intellectual properties.

An additional intellectual property that may attach to a fictional character as portrayed by a particular entertainer is the right of publicity. This property right is often disguised and judicially managed as a personal right of privacy. Although the right of publicity is of limited interest here, it does serve as a conduit to the association of intellectual properties in characters as products in the marketplace. Merchandising may prove to be of far greater significance in the marketplace than the media of character origins. Since this is where the financial stake may ultimately reside, merchandising may also command the bulk of future judicial attention.

In the end, however, copyright remains undeniably the first and foremost property by which characters are legally protected. In this book, I suggest a classification to aid in analysis of the case law. I also propose a formula for reconciliation of the apparently inconsistent judicial decisions applied to characters studied throughout this work. The same formula is proferred as a guide for predicting future judicial outcomes.

Through these tools, I conclude that, despite the silence of the Copyright Act regarding character and characterization, no amendment is in order. There is neither inconsistency nor any gap in legal recognition of fictional characters as intellectual properties. They are fully protected, especially by copyright and the precise drafting of licensing agreements. Some characters, who have caught the public imagination, are further protected through trademark and unfair competition.

In the end, the answer to my opening query is yes. Fictional characters are adequately protected by a combination of all three components of intellectual property—copyright, trademark, and unfair competition.

Part I

INTRODUCTION TO INTELLECTUAL PROPERTY LAW

1

Historical Perspective on Intellectual Properties in the United States

BASIC CONCEPTS OF PROPERTY

Law in the United States can be categorized in a variety of ways.[1] Conceptually, the law may be codified in statutes and regulations, or it may evolve through adjudication at the federal level or in the courts of the several states. Case law frequently centers on the interpretation and application of codified law, as is usually the case with copyright and trademark matters.

The highest statute in the land is the U.S. Constitution. To the extent that it does not derive from the Constitution, all other law must at least be consistent with the Constitution's provisions and, to a certain extent, with the underlying moral precepts.

Statutory law is enacted within our system of federalism; that is, there are certain matters that can only come out of the Congress and others that are in the domain of the states and their numerous subdivisions. Still other matters may be subject to both federal and state legislation. Patents, copyrights, and trademarks are the exclusive province of the federal courts.

The more generic unfair competition, on the other hand, may also be regulated by the states. In cases of unfair competition, federal and state jurisdiction overlap, particularly where trademark law is also at issue. Certain matters which can also be categorized within unfair competition at least for the sake of convenience, may be primarily the province of case law.

Law can also be categorized as procedural or substantive. Procedure is the framework on which matters of legal substance are handled. Substantive law embraces all the subject matter that the legal system is mandated to address. The concept of property is a basic and very ancient precept of substantive law.

Today the courts recognize three kinds of property: real, personal, and intellectual. The term *real estate* reflects the feudal concept of land as the very foundation on which the whole of society was based. Everything from sustenance to resources for defense and for the lord's warfare came from possession of land. Much of English history and literature is based in the feudal concept of real property—the present and future interests or property rights (and duties) associated with land and with buildings or other fixtures.

Both real and personal property have numerous attendant rights and responsibilities. Law professors often represent these "bundles of rights" as analogous to a handful of sticks. For example, ownership of real and personal property can be distinguished from possession; ownership represents the whole bundle of sticks with possession being only one part of the whole. It goes without saying that a landlord has quite a different array of rights, duties, authority, and liabilities than does a tenant. Usually these are spelled out in a contract in the form of a lease. Certain of the rights retained by the owner of land and other rights transferred to the tenant may themselves be transferred in transactions independent of the lease.

It is relatively easy to sort out the corresponding array of legal implications associated with real property. Similarly, different legal principles apply depending on the status of a chattel. Ownership is the most inclusive and gives the strongest property rights. Possession may be the most immediately pragmatic association with property. There are many others, but chattels, unlike land, can be mislaid or lost. Certain rights may be retained when a chattel is mislaid, but when it is lost and perhaps forgotten, abandonment of it and of the rights attaching to it is the ultimate result. Abandoned property can be claimed by anyone who asserts a right over it. It can be said to be in the public domain.

Often these principles are reflected in contracts, such as a contract for the purchase and sale of a horse or a refrigerator or a suit of clothes—frequently the contract is no more complicated than a sales slip. Like land, chattels can also be leased or subjected to other, more sophisticated, formal agreements.

Real property and personal property were concepts easily grasped early in the evolution of Anglo-American law. The concept of intellectual property is more elusive because the property is intangible: ideas and their various forms of expression. As with real and tangible personal property, every object of intellectual property, once manifested, becomes subject to a whole array of legal rights, duties, and liabilities very closely analogous to those associated with the tangible personal properties. Two points are essential: First, the intellectual property must somehow have been rendered tangible (a book, painting, phonograph record, audio- or videotape, computer printout, and so on—subject only to the limitations of human imagination). Second, the associated rights and other principles may be retained or transferred or lost independently of one another, primarily through contractual arrangements, usually licensing agreements. In most senses the law of intellectual property is at the very least reminiscent of the law of tangible personal property, even though the underlying idea and all the so-called properties in it will remain intangible. Trademarks, like personal property, can be abandoned voluntarily by act of the proprietor or, uniquely, involuntarily through public use.

According to legal tradition, case law is further categorized. In England the early courts of law became so bound up in form that the true substance of a case was unfairly lost in the intricacies of the draconian procedural constraints. A separate clerical jurisprudence, administered by the chancellor, arose. Today, cases are still distinguished as being "in law" or "in equity." Cases in equity, such as those involving questions of intellectual property, are characterized by an often titanic mental struggle to find the proper balance within the maze of conflicting rights and duties before the court.

Basic fairness is the key to equity, though lawyers are strangely loath to use the word. "It's not fair" is the unrecognized whine of Everyman at his worst. "It is an inequity" is an articulate plea for justice. Courts will hear only the latter. In this context it is absolutely essential to remember that, when dealing with matters of intellectual property, the minimum number of parties to whom equitable doctrine is being applied at trial is not two but three: in assessing and balancing the rights, if any, to the original property and the liabilities that may be imposed against the proprietor of the allegedly infringing property, the courts will take note of the interests of the public seeking to enjoy one or the other (and sometimes both). This balancing act can become particularly precarious, and indeed takes more than a few odd turns, when popular fictional characters are the properties at issue.

THE *INS v. AP* CASE

In 1918 the United States Supreme Court decided a case entitled *International News Service v. Associated Press.*[2] The case raised three questions: Is there any property in news? If so, does it survive first publication? And, most specifically, did the conduct of the defendant, International News Service (INS), constitute unfair competition?

These questions of property rights were not subject to the law of copyright because of the unique nature of news. Instead, the plaintiff, Associated Press (AP), was asking the court to make an analogy to literary property within the existing law of copyright in order to acknowledge a comparable right of property in news.

The two parties to the lawsuit were competitors in the gathering and distribution of news and its publication for profit in U.S. newspapers. The cost to the plaintiff of providing this service was $3.5 million per year, no small figure in 1918. Naturally there were limits on the use to which the customers of Associated Press could put the news items provided. Both the two services and most of their respective customers were in keen competition. Moreover, that competition was direct, and the value of the service provided depended in part upon speed of transmission. Implicit in their competition was the effort to avoid being "scooped." The plaintiff, therefore, sought to restrain by court order certain actions on the part of the defendant that AP considered to be improper.

The federal district court entered an order prior to going to trial. That order restrained two of the three activities in which International News Service was participating, but it did not restrain the copying of news items for sale by the defendant. The federal court of appeals sustained the order of the trial court and remanded the question of copying to that lower court for a determination of whether the copying usurped some property right in news and thus constituted unfair competition in violation of the law.

The Supreme Court acknowledged an intellectual property in news in its affirmation of the appellate court's remand—but not without a struggle. The first point the high court made was that the issue was one of unfair competition, a matter subject to federal case law rather than that of the various states or the federal Copyright Act. In considering the nature of any property in the news, the high court observed that its substance must be distinguished from the form of communication: words. The value of this property lies in spreading the news while it is fresh.

The Supreme Court carefully distinguished the property rights existing between each party and the public and those existing between one party and the other: Neither party had any property interest as against the public in uncopyrighted news following first publication. It did not follow, however, that there was no remaining property interest in that news as between the competing parties. Such news can be regarded simply as the material out of which both parties were seeking to make profits at the same time and in the same field. For this limited purpose and between those parties, the Supreme Court accepted such news as quasi-property, without regard for any rights of either party as against the public.[3]

Amidst much discussion the Supreme Court held that the

defendant's acts ultimately amounted to an unauthorized interference with the normal operation of the plaintiff's legitimate business. Moreover, that interference intruded precisely at the point where the profit was to be reaped. The defendant's acts diverted a material portion of the profit from those who had earned it to those who had not, with a particular advantage accruing to the defendant in the competition precisely because the defendant was not burdened with any part of the expense of gathering the news. The transaction was clearly and properly characterized as unfair competition in business.[4]

The Supreme Court pointedly observed that the decision did not confer on Associated Press a monopoly right over either the gathering or the distribution of news or even the right to prevent the reproduction of articles not protected by copyright. The decision served only to postpone the competitor's participation in those activities where it had not gathered the news on its own. Moreover the protection is provided only to the extent "necessary to prevent that competitor from reaping the fruits of complainant's efforts and expenditure, to the partial exclusion of complainant, and in violation of the principle that underlies the maxim" requiring each person to use property in such a way as not to injure the property of another.[5]

More than one justice dissented. The dissenting position was that the controversy involved no property in the first place. Hence, one dissenting justice argued that it would be sufficient for INS to acknowledge its source, AP. A second dissenting opinion consisted of a highly philosophical dissertation, illustrative of not only the nature of intellectual property but also the ways of judicial reasoning in this particular context. This opinion stated that exclusive enjoyment is essential to individual property, but that right can be absolute only when it is private. Whenever a public interest is present, that right to exclusion is qualified.

Costs in and value of a product of the mind, then, are insufficient to ensure exclusivity. Generally, under the law, knowledge, ascertained truths, and ideas all enter into the public domain once voluntarily imparted.

Certain creations of the mind are protected, but only pursuant to the Copyright Act or patent law. Similarly, theories of contract or of unfair competition can confer qualified protection as against the defendant only.[6]

The dissenting opinions in *INS v. AP* also reveal certain of the limitations of the copyright law and distinguish legal from moral principles, not to mention practical limitations on the judiciary, particularly including the perceived inability to devise a remedy to redress a novel wrong.[7] All of these points are particularly worthy of note in this context of protecting popular literary properties or, more specifically, fictional characters.

Of particular interest here is the dissent's distinction between impropriety denounced by society and wrongs recognized and sanctioned under the law. In 1914 appropriation for profit of another's knowledge or ideas might have been inconsistent with morality but it had not been sanctioned by law. Not so much as compensation or even acknowledgement had been demanded to date.[8]

It is helpful, then, to accept at the outset that plagiarism may be immoral, but it is not necessarily infringement. While the courts stop short of actually condoning plagiarism, infringement is the only recognized *legal* wrong that the courts can act to prevent or halt.

STATUTORY PROTECTION OF INTELLECTUAL PROPERTY

Constitutional Protection of Intellectual Property

In the United States, all analyses of intellectual property rights must start with the highest law in the land, the U.S. Constitution. Section 8 of Article I charges the legislative branch with the regulation of commerce and with the promotion of "the Progress of Science and the useful Arts, by securing for limited Times to Authors and Inventors the exclusive Right to their respective Writings and Discoveries." (It is both proper and highly informative to read "monopoly" in place of "exclusive Right.") These exclusive rights take the form of patents, copyrights, and trademarks.

Patent, Copyright, and Trademark

Definitions.[9] A patent is defined as a "grant made by the government to an inventor, conveying to him the exclusive right to make, use and sell his invention for a term of years." Patents will not be discussed here, except as contrasting with copyright or trademarks.

Copyright is defined as an "intangible, incorporeal right granted by statute to the author or originator of certain literary or artistic productions, whereby he is invested, for a limited period, with the sole and exclusive privilege of multiplying copies of the same and publishing and selling them." A major part of this book's discussions will center on copyrights.

Trademark is not so easily defined. A good starting point, however, is "a distinctive mark of authenticity, through which the products of particular manufacturers or the vendible commodities of particular merchants may be distinguished from those of others." The Lanham Act defines this property to include "any word, name, symbol or device or any combination thereof adopted and used by a manufacturer or merchant to identify his goods and distinguish them from those sold by others." Such a mark is deemed abandoned when "any course of conduct of the registrant, including acts of omission as well as commission, causes the mark to lose its significance as an indication of origin."[10]

This book will be looking closely at trademarks only where they overlap with copyright, a most interesting aspect of unfair competition. In this context unfair competition refers to "dishonest or fraudulant rivalry in trade and commerce, . . . particularly [as] applied in the courts of equity . . . to the practice of endeavoring to substitute one's own goods or products in the markets for those of another, having an established reputation and extensive sales."

Copyright.[11] Copyright traces its ancestry to the Statute of Anne, enacted in 1710 by the British Parliament. The legislatures of the several newly created states followed the British lead until superseded by the Constitution. The first federal copyright statute was enacted in 1790 with revisions in 1831,

1870, and 1909. In 1976 there was a major revision of the Copyright Act,[12] which presently remains in effect.

In the simplest terms, a copyright (wholly dependent upon the provisions of the federal act) is equated to the author's right to multiply his literary and intellectual productions and still retain his monopoly therein after publication.[13] In fact, it is a relatively simple matter to copyright or to register a copyright in an appropriate original work of art—whether written, composed, sculpted, painted, or created in some novel tangible form. One need only review the straightforward registration form to do so. The complications arise elsewhere.

Trademark. A trademark gives its proprietor the right to prohibit its use, but only to the extent necessary to protect the proprietor's good will against the sale of another's product as his. The purpose of the Lanham Act's protection of trademarks is to prevent one person from passing off his own goods as those of another. Deception or public confusion is a necessary element of a case in trademark infringement.[14] Here the act that constitutes unfair competition is the misrepresentation to the public: "The infringement of a trademark consists in its use or imitation by another of his goods in such manner that the purchasers of such goods are deceived, or liable to be deceived, and induced to believe that they were manufactured or sold by the owner of the trademark."[15]

Like a copyright, a trademark may be registered, but it is not a property in quite the same sense. Instead, trademark serves the threefold purpose of protection of the public and of the proprietor's goodwill and his reputation. The latter two are decidedly of secondary concern. Most important, a trademark indicates origin or source of a specific product. It serves as a guarantee of a specific level of quality.[16]

Distinctions among intellectual properties. In intellectual property cases, the distinction of copyright properties from those protected by patent or trademark can be confusing. It is helpful to accept the following synopsis:

> [The] law requires that a work be the product of your own mind in order to be copyrightable. Originality is not by itself sufficient; facts,

even if they are facts that no one else has ever discovered, are regarded as the common property of all of us, as are scientific discoveries, mathematical equations, and historical theories. Facts are not copyrightable because they are not human inventions; theories are not copyrightable because they are ideas, not expression. But although originality is not sufficient in itself, it is essential all the same.[17]

But originality of expression in an appropriate medium is all that is necessary.

The best starting point for analysis of copyright protection is reference to the statute itself. The statute recognizes seven categories (media) of property as appropriate: (1) literary works; (2) musical works (including lyrics); (3) dramatic works (including music); (4) pantomimes and choreographic works; (5) pictorial, graphic, and sculptural works; (6) motion pictures and other audiovisual works; and (7) sound recordings.[18] Ownership of the copyright in these various works is to be distinguished from the ownership of any corresponding *material* object subject to the copyright.[19] It is essential to keep in mind that

> copyright is in reality a bundle of rights, each of which may be exploited separately.... The author may transfer any one or more of them without transferring the others. The owner or exclusive licensee of any of these rights is, with respect to that right, a "copyright owner." He is like a tenant who can sublet to a third person and collect rent from the subtenant.[20]

It should be obvious that the individual who buys a copy of a novel acquires no part of the associated intellectual property embodied in its copyright. The individual owns only the volume purchased. Similarly, purchase of a videotape conveys no more than the right to view it at your leisure in the privacy of your own home.

Copyright is associated with seven media of expression, but what exactly are the rights comprising this intellectual property? The statute expressly confers five rights: (1) to reproduce in copies or phonorecords, (2) to prepare derivative works, (3) to distribute copies or phonorecords to the public by sale or other means of transfer, (4) to perform the work publicly, and

(5) with special but not exclusive reference to graphics and films, to display the work publicly.[21] In the event any of these rights is infringed, the proprietor is entitled to appropriate injunctions and the impoundment and disposition of the infringing articles.[22] Note that there is no reference to characters in the statutory provision.

The courts have expanded statutory coverage to include the plot of a novel, at least so far as it is original with the author. Although fictional characters have been the frequent subject of litigation, the extent of their protection, according to observers, remains in a state of confusion.[23] It is the purpose of this work to eliminate the confusion. To do so, however, requires a thorough background in the intellectual properties that can attach to characters. Chapter 2 is the starting point, beginning with copyright itself.

NOTES

1. For discussions of basic principles of law, *see, e.g.*, M. RADIN, ANGLO-AMERICAN HISTORY (1936), H. GRILLIOT, INTRODUCTION TO LAW AND THE LEGAL SYSTEM (3d ed. 1983), G. CLARKE, SUMMARY OF AMERICAN LAW (1949); for basics of intellectual property, *see, e.g.*, M. EPSTEIN, MODERN INTELLECTUAL PROPERTY (1984).
2. International News Service v. Associated Press, 248 U.S. 215, 39 S. Ct. 68, 63 L. Ed. 211 (1918).
3. 39 S. Ct. at 71.
4. 39 S. Ct. at 72–73.
5. 39 S. Ct. at 73.
6. 39 S. Ct. at 76.
7. 39 S. Ct. at 78.
8. 39 S. Ct. at 79, 82.
9. All definitions in this section are from BLACK'S LAW DICTIONARY, (rev. 4th ed. 1968), unless otherwise noted.
10. 15 U.S.C. 1051, at §1127.
11. This brief history is taken from Wilson, *Visual Arts & the Law*, in LAW AND THE ARTS/ART AND THE LAW (T. HORWITZ, ed. 1979). *See also* W. STRONG, THE COPYRIGHT BOOK/A PRACTICAL GUIDE (2d ed. 1984).
12. 17 U.S.C. 101 *et seq.*, as amended in 1976 by Pub. L. 94–553.
13. 18 AM. JUR. 2d, *Copyright* §80 (1965).
14. 74 AM. JUR. 2d, *Trademarks and Tradenames* §84 (1974).

15. 74 AM. JUR. 2d, *Trademarks and Tradenames* §85 (1974, citation omitted).

16. Taken from the Chicago Bar Association's March 1982 seminar, Intellectual Property for Non-Specialists.

17. STRONG, *supra* note 11, at 3 (citation omitted). *Also see* Saidman, *Copyrights: Novelty or originality*? 55 J. PAT. OFF. SOC'Y 314 (1973), at 322.

Note that patent, the one category of intellectual property I will not be addressing, is distinguished by three characteristics: novelty, originality, and usefulness.

18. 17 U.S.C. 102(a).

19. 17 U.S.C. 202.

20. STRONG, *supra* note 11, at 36.

21. 17 U.S.C. 106.

22. 17 U.S.C. 501–504.

23. STRONG, *supra* note 11, at 16–18.

2

Copyright Protection in the Courts: The Elements of an Infringement Action

PRINCIPLES OF COPYRIGHT PROTECTION

Legal cases concerning copyright reveal that copyright infringement first requires the existence of an original work both subject to copyright and duly copyrighted. The content of the work must be of a nature generally recognized as a property subject to copyright and, more specifically, must be an expression expanding upon the underlying idea. Infringement involves an unauthorized taking of the expression by which the idea was conveyed in the original work. The mere taking of an idea is never sufficient to support an infringement action.

The most obvious infringement is outright plagiarism—direct copying—of the original expression. Most often, however, so obvious an appropriation cannot be demonstrated. Instead, infringement must be inferred from a showing of the defendant's access to the plaintiff's work and of substantial similarity in the expression of the two works.

As a preliminary matter, on one hand, certain categories of works are in the public domain ab initio; e.g., facts, especially historical facts. On the other hand, the allegedly infringing material may actually come from an independent source. In neither case does an infringement action lie. Given neither of these circumstances, analysis usually turns to access and a comparison of expression. Most cases of copyright infringement actually turn on the matter of substantial similarity, based on a test of ordinary observation. In this chapter, the review of case law will focus on the question of substantial similarity in preparation for analyses of cases in which character protection is a prominent feature.

APPLICATION OF PRINCIPLES

Sources of the Works

Fact or embellishment. The necessary distinction between uncopyrightable historical fact and material subject to copyright protection is illustrated in a case involving documentary films of the Russian Revolution.[1] The plaintiff collected his documentary films during the interval of 1917 through 1930, recording the actual historical events in a 1937 film, *Tsar to Lenin*, which was copyrighted. The defendant, a Russian, produced a similar body of work. Eventually he licensed a portion of this work, *Halfway to Hell*, to NBC for television and theatrical release and as a weekly series, *Background to Battle*.

It should come as no surprise that the films of the plaintiff and the defendant contained some identical footage. The result was a charge of copyright infringement and unfair competition and a counterclaim for libel.[2]

In resolving the question of infringement, the U.S. Court of Appeals for the Ninth Circuit acknowledged that, while historical events recorded by both parties were, as history, in the public domain, there still could be a copyright in the surrounding contribution of the "author" of the film. To that extent the plaintiff's film could indeed be protected from infringement. The court went on to reason that there were three points at which the author's contributions would be subject to infringement: sequential development, commentary, and mapping. The court proceeded to look for evidence of the defendant's access to the plaintiff's work and of similarities in expression at those three points, where the plaintiff would be protected. (The question of similarity ordinarily involves analysis of the competing works to determine whether copying has followed access. But, it should be noted, similarity can also resolve the question of the sources of the two works.)

On the basis of these analyses and with express reference to the activities resulting in the *INS* litigation, reported in chapter 1, the court held that this situation was factually distinguishable from that of the earlier case. Unlike the defendant INS, the defendant here had produced his work independently, albeit working from the same facts as the plaintiff. Thus, there could be no infringement.

Just as historical fact is in the public domain and, as such, outside copyright protection, so too is research, at least according to one circuit.[3] According to the Southern District of New York, such cases can turn on whether material is news reporting; that is, factual. This district has held that the contents of former President Ford's memoirs dealing with Nixon's pardon are not to be deemed news; therefore, an article based on those contents infringed the copyrighted memoirs.[4]

In the context of applications to popular works, it is worth noting four practical factors influencing this decision in the New York district:

Intent: The defendant's work was published for profit.

Timing: The infringed work was soon to be published.

Degree of taking: The defendant took the "heart" of the book.

Practical result: The infringing publication caused another publishing agreement to be aborted, thus diminishing the value of the plaintiff's copyright.[5]

Sources of fictional works. In determining whether the play, *Death Takes a Holiday*, was an infringement of the copyrighted play, *Most*, the Southern District of New York, after summarizing the two works, accepted the defendant's claim that *Death Takes a Holiday* was actually a translation of a third work, the Italian *La Morte in Vacanze*.[6] Thus, although access was deemed likely because the plaintiff's work preceded the defendant's by some twenty years and was distributed in the theatrical community, there was no infringement. In so deciding, the court relied on "ordinary observation," judging the work as it was, not as the author would interpret it.

A common feature of these and all copyright cases is, then, an attempt to identify actual sources; sometimes of the plaintiff's work and always of the defendant's work. Only when this initial matter is resolved in favor of the plaintiff, will a court turn to an analysis of the competing works.

Access and Substantial Similarity

As noted, an action for infringement of copyright requires that the allegedly infringing work be taken from another's work without permission. This element is most often demonstrated through substantial similarity in the expression of the idea common to the two works subject to the controversy. This is the primary point of departure in proceeding from the statutory provisions into resolution of actual controversies.

It is the judicial application of equitable principles under the direction provided by the Copyright Act that resolves the actual controversies. The resolution tends to be fairly straightforward when only one medium is involved, although an occasional complication does set in even here. Additional complications are always superimposed when different media are involved.

Literary media. The question of infringement can arise even before a work is published in the commercial sense. The author of an unpublished novel, *Return from Nowhere*, sued the publisher of the novel *Ghost Boat* for infringement of common law copyright[7] (recognized by the current statute although registration is a prerequisite to an infringement action).[8] The case was on appeal from a summary judgment for the defendant. Although the two works both centered on the concept of a lost vessel of World War II resurfacing some thirty years later, the lower court had found no similarity of the expression.

The published work was a tale of the supernatural delving into the Bermuda Triangle lore popular at that time. In the unpublished work the supernatural event merely served as the vehicle for a study of the crew's attempts to adjust to the modern world. Here the appellate court agreed with the trial court: the ordinary reasonable person would find no similarity of expression and only a remote resemblance of the ideas.

In a second case, a judgment of infringement in similar circumstances was affirmed.[9] Here, the plaintiff submitted a manuscript, *Pirate Queen of Connaught,* to the defendant publisher. The defendant held it approximately one month and advised that its juvenile department might have some interest. Apparently, at the same time *Pirate Queen*—the work ultimately published—was also being considered. Although agents of the publisher denied even reading the plaintiff's unpublished manuscript, the trial court exercised its judicial discretion in finding to the contrary. The appellate court agreed.

Both works involved a historical character about whom few facts are known. The crucial point, and the one clearly distinguishing this from the preceding case, is that there were similarities in the *fictional* aspects of the two works. It could, of course, have been no more than coincidence, but two courts thought coincidence an unlikely explanation.

The appropriation of unpublished manuscripts is of particular concern to the novice author. There are in fact two possible actions under these circumstances: tortious interference with a literary property right and breach of fiduciary duties, both of which were unsuccessfully raised in a case of common law copyright before the courts of Illinois.[10]

Several points raised by this case are worth noting. First, the plaintiff was in the business of producing audiovisual programs and actually produced and distributed the allegedly infringed program with the defendant. Moreover, the underlying contract allowed the defendant to terminate the program, and the defendant had paid all that was owed under the contract.

There was a directed verdict for the defendant on the issue of tortious interference, suggesting that the facts did not support this as a legitimate cause of action. The claimed breach of fiduciary relationship was rejected only when the lower court refused to allow the plaintiff to amend the complaint, also suggesting the basic theoretical viability of this legal theory.

A more successful outcome occurred in a California case.[11] The theories advanced were plagiarism, quasi contract, breach of implied contract, and breach of fiduciary or confidential relationship, and so forth. The theory on which the trial proceeded was breach of implied contract.

The results of these cases make it clear that a creative artist must take extreme care in the drafting of contracts conveying literary properties.[12] This will also be illustrated in chapter 7 through the series of cases brought by Edgar Rice Burroughs, Inc. against MGM.

Upon publication a commercially successful work can come to legal grief. The novel *Rebecca* by Daphne Du Maurier was alleged to be an infringement of the magazine story *I Planned to Murder My Husband* and the novel *Blind Windows*.[13] The district court found for the defendant on the basis of the pleadings. The plaintiff's works were described as involving an ordinary love triangle seen from the point of view of a second wife and ending in the death of the husband. *Rebecca*, of course, is far more sophisticated in concept and in execution.

The trial court based this decision on the fact that the stories were clearly dissimilar despite the similarities raised by the plaintiff. In short, it was found that, as a matter of law, there was no substantial copying of the plaintiff's protected material. No additional factual development was required. The Second Circuit disagreed.

It held that a trial of the issues must proceed to determine the extent to which material was borrowed for *Rebecca* and whether any material common to both works was within the protection of the copyright law. The majority view of this appellate court tended to hold in little esteem the allegation of copying but still insisted that nothing was known of Du Maurier's access to the plaintiff's material. Further, what supporting evidence of copying the plaintiff could produce had gone unanswered. In fact, both of these issues had been conceded for purposes of the motion. Acceptance of that concession precluded dismissal of the complaint.[14]

There was an articulate dissent bearing more than a tinge of judicial indignation:

> I must consider it as bordering rather on the fantastic, as implying callousness towards, if not derision of, real literary talent and skill, to suggest that such trifling and coincidental similarities as a micro-

scopic examination of the two books is thought to bring out here be considered to weigh at all against the sharp differences between them in all matters which really should count—viz., in intended objective and type of reader appeal, in fashioning of the plot and in its progression, in the conception and delineation of characters, in the climax of the story and denoument of the plot, and in the effectiveness and, certainly in part at least, in the literary skill with which the chosen objective is reached.[15]

On the one hand, we have an attempted psychoanalytical study (in not too successful imitation of a recent vogue in novels) of a young girl through her childhood and down through her unsuccessful marriage to an older man previously married; as might be expected, the biography merely runs on without climax until the book closes sometime after the husband has died and as the heroine seemingly contemplates return to an earlier love. On the other hand, we have a superbly fashioned melodrama—told, it is true, by a second wife—of suspense and horror cleverly combined, wherein the hero's first wife is the villain and the denoument is sharp and unusual, leading directly to the close of the book, with the hero and heroine having lost their home in flames, but obviously about to live happily ever after.[16] I believe the courts do a disservice to literature to encourage the harassment which such a trial means, with its obvious tendency to force settlement of the claim not because it is just, but because contesting it has become too costly or too inconvenient.[17]

Art and music. Needless to say, the written word is far from the sole source of infringement actions. Given the number of media subject to copyright law and given the irrepressible entrepreneurial spirit provoking the marketing of popular properties in every conceivable format, an impressive array of intra- and intermedium infringements is inevitable.

The initial question is always that of applicability of copyright. A case involving lamp bases formed from china statuettes of dancing male and female figures made it all the way to the Supreme Court on that very question.[18] The appellate court had reversed the dismissal of the complaint. The Supreme Court responded in the affirmative as to the applicability of copyright to a lamp base statuette. With that determination, the matter was remanded for trial for application of pertinent copyright analyses to the competing statuettes. In remanding, the Supreme Court reiterated the established doctrine that copyright, as contrasted with patent, protects the expression, not the idea. In further contrast with patent, copyright protects only originality in expression. Copyright embraces neither novelty nor invention, and its protection confers only the exclusive right of multiplying copies, or reproduction.

Given the nature of copyright protection, it is quite possible for the work of an author to infringe another work by the same author. An example is found in two paintings by a single artist. The artist of *Cardinals on Apple Blossom* transferred all reproduction rights in the copyrighted painting to the National Wildlife Art Exchange. Subsequently, the artist did four watercolors of birds for the Franklin Mint. One of the group was called *The Cardinal* and relied on some of the same source materials previously used for *Cardinals on Apple Blossom*. Although the earlier copyright was valid, the appellate court affirmed the finding that the earlier work per se had not been copied.[19]

Although the composition of the new painting was found to be different, the proper resolution of the case was no simple matter. The appellate court struggled with the elusive boundary between the unprotected idea and its protected expression. The court noted the corresponding blurring between copying and appropriation. Then it observed the added complication of applying the same general principles to claims arising from plays, novels, sculptures, maps, information directories, and musical compositions, along with paintings.

Indeed, this court accepted the principle that isolating the idea from the expression and determining the extent of copying required for unlawful appropriation necessarily depend, at least to some degree, on whether the subject matter is words or symbols written on paper or paint brushed on canvas.[20] In other words, the medium or media of expression will demand some differences in the requisite legal analyses.

Ultimately, the court was able to distinguish the expression from the idea, while also resolving the inevitable tension between conflicting rights of copyright monopoly versus freedom of expression. The defendant, Franklin Mint, had relied upon "variations on a theme" as analogous to the freedom that must be extended to artists to utilize basic subject matter more than once. The plaintiff, on the other hand, asserted that such a concept is contrary to the very theory of copyright. The court reasoned that a variation probably is not a copy, and if a theme is equated with an idea, it may not be monopolized. In short, a variation on a theme is another way of saying that an idea may not be copyrighted and only its expression may be protected.[21]

Among the most problematic subjects of copyright is music. Comprehension of music theory and precise technical analyses are prerequisites to adequate comparison of competing musical compositions. There have been, as might be expected, numerous cases involving popular music. One early case involves two familiar names: Nicky Arnstein and Cole Porter.[22] Arnstein was appealing the summary dismissal of his complaint charging Porter with a variety of copyright abuses in certain of Porter's most familiar compositions.

Defendant Porter categorically denied seeing or hearing any of the plaintiff's works. Thus the factual questions of copying and of improper appropriation were raised. The appellate court ruled that, when some similarity is found, the summary judgment is proper only where the plaintiff's work was without doubt inaccessible to the defendant. This case was remanded to put Porter's credibility to a jury. Once again there was a dissent, this time based on musical analysis.

Dramatic arts. The cinema provides one of the most fascinating areas of intellectual property. While many screenplays are entirely original, the cinema traditionally has turned to history and literature for inspiration. The transformation to film from literature and other media is fraught with difficulties—for all the memorable successes. Often the feel or theme of the source is retained or lost quite independently of the characters, plot, or events being dramatized. Except for any underlying formalities the law is not invoked when the taking is legitimate—only the art of criticism.

There are three broad areas in which the law of copyright infringement can enter the scene when the taking is less than completely legitimate: in the transformation from another medium into film, between films, and from film into another medium. The transformed products are known as "derivative works." Each is directly derived from—recast, transformed, or adapted from—an earlier creation.[23] Obviously, such derivative works may or may not be authorized by the holder of the copyright in the original creation. If not authorized, infringement may have occurred.

Two essential legal distinctions apply here. How is expression to be extracted from idea in the original creation? Then, when a new creation conveys a similar idea, at what point does its expression sufficiently depart from that of the original to avoid constituting actionable infringement? This, in fact, is the very essence of the analysis of similarity for purposes of copyright protection.

It is helpful to keep in mind that protection of a derivative work itself will extend only to those of its components that comprise the original contribution of its creator.[24] But what of the original creation? When is a derivative work an infringing copy and when can it stand as an independent creation? Clearly *derivative* can be used in two senses: the popular term acknowledging a relationship between two works and the legal term of art. A work the public recognizes as derivative may or may not represent an actionable infringement of its most likely predecessor.

Examination of specific works in the popular media serves to clarify this crucial distinction. For example, the musical *West Side Story* is not derivative of *Romeo and Juliet* in the sense that the film *Gone with the Wind* is derivative of Margaret Mitchell's novel of the same name. Although inspired by Shakespeare's classic, *West Side Story* does not simply retell the story in a different medium. Instead, it tells its own story, which resembles Shakespeare's drama in many significant respects.[25] That an unauthorized cinematic *Gone with the Wind* would infringe Mitchell's novel is virtually a legal certainty. By contrast, the hypothetical legal relationship between *West Side Story* and Shakespeare's great romantic tragedy is somewhat less clear, although more than one commentator asserts that the former would be actionably derivative.[26] It would be a close call, in part dependent upon any licensing negotiations between the two authors prior to the advent of *West Side Story*. The complexity of this type of case is further examined through the discussion of defenses to copyright infringement in the next chapter.

The kinds of complications that can arise are illustrated in the creative pathway by which the film *South Pacific* derives from James Michener's stories, *Tales of the South Pacific*. The intervening adaptations consisted of a musical combining and adapting the stories and a screenplay rewritten from the musical. Three layers of derivative works are present. Each cut some material and added its own. Three different copyrights preceded that of the film itself.[27] While a court might readily find sufficient similarities to support copyright infringement in moving from screenplay to film or even from musical to film, considerably more scrutiny would be required to connect the film to the stories, were that connection not memorialized in the associated licensing documents. In cases involving books translated to film, results from one jurisdiction to another might well be at variance.

Now that a framework has been provided, judicial analyses of pertinent principles may more readily be reconciled in preparation for addressing the application of these principles to fictional characters. The initial step was to recognize motion picture rights in popular literary properties.

When the film *Ben-Hur* was introduced in 1907, motion picture rights did not yet exist. Infringement actions did. Both the publishers of the novel and the producers of the stage dramatization sued, and *Ben-Hur* was withdrawn from distribution in 1911 with $25,000 being tendered to the victors. Subsequently, motion picture rights came to be recognized by law, and in 1922 the stage producers were convinced to allow the transfer to the screen.

Quo Vadis? was published in 1895. When the first cinema version, with a running time of less than a half hour, was made in 1901, it apparently never occurred to the author to act on his copyright. When he did act on the 1910 version, the film was simply retitled and released—successfully. The author, Henryk Sienkiewicz, did sell the rights for the 1912 version. Since then *Quo Vadis?* has been remade in 1924 and 1950.[28]

A far more complicated story is associated with the motion picture rights for the opera *Madame Butterfly*.[29] This work has enjoyed numerous incarnations beginning with the novel written in 1897. The case for declaratory judgment and injunction, decided in the early 1950s, is a graphic illustration of the problems surrounding derivative works. It further illustrates an integral relationship between copyright and contractual arrangements in distributing copyright properties from medium to medium

The novel, *Madame Butterfly*, was written and copyrighted in 1897. An authorized drama was written in 1900 and copyrighted in 1917. By a 1901 contract granting exclusive rights, the opera's libretto was created and copyrighted in 1904. All copyrights were renewed with the exception of the 1900 drama. Its copyright expired in 1945 and was never renewed. The plaintiff was claiming motion pictures rights through the libretto, while the defendant was claiming the same rights through the novel and drama. The defendant asserted that the plaintiff required consent to proceed with a film, because the plaintiff's exclusive rights had terminated with expirations of copyright in the novel and drama.

The Second Circuit found no need to explore the details of the contractual arrangements but reasoned on the basis of copyright principles. First, it was held that the libretto was subject to an independent copyright that was unaffected by the fate of copyright in the novel. The plaintiff's rights were, however, limited to material which was new to the libretto. The plaintiff was not authorized to incorporate material from the novel in a film.

Next, the drama was found to be in the public domain. Both the plaintiff and the defendant were entitled to draw upon it as a source. To the extent that the defendant's exclusive rights depended on the drama, they had expired in 1945 with its copyright. Thus, to the extent that the plaintiff drew material from the libretto supplemented by material from the drama without returning to the novel itself, the film could proceed without the defendant's consent.

In considering adaptations to film from the written word, it is worth noting that the courts were not slow to recognize that a film can infringe without use of the infringed work's dialogue. Were this not the case, according to the Second Circuit, there could be no piracy of a pantomime. Here there can be no dialogue, but the art of pantomime is clearly a form of drama. Speech, after all, is but one small part of a dramatist's means of expression. Drama draws on all the arts and is fabricated from words, gestures, scenery, and costumes and from the very looks of the actors themselves. From time to time any dramatic piece may lapse into pantomime, and these moments may actually be the most poignant and significant, however subtle the means of expressing them. Because a drama is "the sequence of the confluents of all these means, bound together in an inseparable unity; it may often be most effectively pirated by leaving out the speech, for which a substitute can be found."[30]

Following the initial interval of naiveté regarding copyright protection, contemporary creative artists, representing all the media, seem far more alert to takings than were their predecessors. One such artist has made an (unsuccessful) attempt to secure a judgment on the basis of infringement by the television series *Kaz* of his story of becoming a "jail house" lawyer or of a three-page summary of that story.[31] While acknowledging certain close similarities, the California district court repeated yet again that the plaintiff must be able to prove either direct copying or access plus substantial similarity. Here the former did not exist and the latter was limited to ideas, locale, themes, or characters: all conceptions, according to this district, not protected by copyright. Moreover, the series, *Kaz*, was found to begin where the plaintiff's work ended, upon becoming an attorney.

As was already observed in the context of authors in search of a publisher, there is a great deal of vulnerability associated with the review of materials submitted for use in the cinema. In a case similar to that involving *Kaz*, the author of a magazine story ("Cupid Rides the Rails") and a related unpublished manuscript (*Old John Santa Fe*) discussed a film adaptation with the Fred Harvey restaurant chain, the Santa Fe Railroad, and Paramount Studios. The idea was rejected. Subsequently, a novel, *The Harvey Girls*, was published and a musical-comedy film of the same name was produced.[32]

The plaintiff focused his infringement action on the film. All his allegations were rejected, and it was held that the basic material was historical and thus in the public domain. In addressing questions of similarity, the test to be applied, according to this circuit, focuses on the impressions of the ordinary observer rather than on some dissection of sentences and incidents in search of seeming similarities.

In another case, it was alleged that a TV production and the subsequent magazine publication of the material at issue were derivative and, thus, infringements of a children's storybook.[33] Despite finding substantial similarity, the trial court dismissed the action with the observation that the works came from the same original source, which was in the public domain. The Second Circuit agreed with the result, but it found no substantial similarity and, therefore, found that the subsequent works were not derivative in any case.

The appellate court based its reasoning on the crucial difference between ideas and the expression of ideas and addressed the conflict that is at least implicit in cases of copyright infringement: the reconciliation of "two competing societal interests: rewarding an individual's ingenuity and effort while at the same time permitting the nation to benefit from further improvements or progress resulting from others' use of the same subject matter."[34]

Author Ray Bradbury did succeed in establishing his case against *A Sound of Different Drummers*, a film alleged to have been taken from his works, "The Fireman" and *Fahrenheit 451*.[35] Reversing the trial court's judgment for the defendants, the appellate court held that the denial of copying did not serve to counter the evidence of both access and similarities. Plaintiff Bradbury cited twenty-two similarities leading the court to observe that it was apparent any ordinary person, after reading either of Bradbury's works and seeing the film, would note similarities suggesting that the film is a dramatization or adaptation of *Fahrenheit 451*.

Specifically, the incidents and their sequence comprising the story line in each of the works are simply too similar to be coincidental. The court refused to accept that the scriptwriter would have incorporated into his work such a number of similar and parallel incidents, episodes, and scenes without access to Bradbury's material. The similarities in question were held to be novel—even strange and unusual—in Bradbury's story. The conclusion followed that the defendants not only copied the theme and ideas of Bradbury's copyrighted work but also its expression.[36]

Since it is often difficult for the layman to figure out how a book and a film are related when they are supposedly "the same," it is not surprising to find it no easy task for courts to determine whether a film has been improperly taken from the written word. Seemingly, the determination would be facilitated when two films are to be compared.

The trial court had no difficulty at all in reaching the conclusion that the film *Great White (The Last Jaws)* was an infringement on *Jaws* and *Jaws II*.[37] No doubt the subtitle was not without significant impact on the decision. The court entered a rare preliminary injunction and ordered the infringing film impounded.

This court obviously found very little that was not substantially similar even though the films were not actually identical. The court noted that the defendants had captured the total concept and feel of *Jaws* and inferred the defendants' intent; namely, to be closely connected with *Jaws*. Two points should be noted at least parenthetically: (1) the ephemeral nature of most film runs, leading to particular damage where there is a contemporaneous release of an infringing property, and (2) the relative simplicity of plot and characterization imposed by this medium as contrasted to most novels.

As soon as the cinema was adopted by television, new rights came to the fore. For example, one case turned on the fate of television rights where film rights had been assigned.[38] (The property, *Maytime*, had certainly made the rounds: to an individual who assigned it to Warner Bros., who in turn assigned it to MGM, who produced the film and subsequently licensed it to television.) Once a film is produced, it is a property subject to legal and illicit adaptation into an astonishing array of media, witness the marketing phenomena to be discussed in chapter 8.

Synthesis: The Extrinsic and Intrinsic Tests

It was the Ninth Circuit that synthesized the elements of a copyright action and fully articulated the distinctions between similarity in idea and in expression.[39] The plaintiffs, puppeteers Sid and Marty Krofft, had created a children's television series known as *H. R. Pufnstuf*. The popularity of the series led to lines of Pufnstuf products and endorsements.

A McDonald's advertising agent approached the Kroffts to join in an advertising campaign using Pufnstuf as a source. Negotiations for the usage in anticipation of a fee went forward until the plaintiffs were advised that the campaign had been cancelled. In fact, however, it was continuing. McDonald's hired former Krofft employees to design and construct costumes and sets and retained the same expert to establish character voices as had the plaintiffs. In time the commercials were broadcast on network television.

Prior to the McDonald's campaign, the plaintiffs had been licensing toys, games, lunch boxes, and comic books. They also licensed cereal commercials, and the Ice Capades had adapted their material. Once McDonald's campaign was launched, however, the plaintiffs were unable to obtain new licensing or to extend existing licenses. The Ice Capades went so far as to replace Pufnstuf characters with those from McDonaldland.

The Kroffts successfully sued for copyright infringement. Cross appeals followed. The defendants argued the lack of infringement as a matter of law, while the plaintiffs were dissatisfied with the amount of damages.

Infringement of both television episodes and articles of merchandise was alleged. The matter went to a jury, which was shown examples of relevant materials. The jury found substantial similarities, and the appellate court declined to hold the verdict clearly erroneous, despite the possibility that each individual element of similarity might be trivial. It was proper, according to the Ninth Circuit, to examine the overall impact and effect.

Acknowledging the competing social interests of rewarding creativity and effort while permitting the nation to enjoy benefits and progress within the subject matter, the appellate court engaged in a close examination of the elements of copyright infringement. Assuming the existence of properly copyrighted material and ownership of the copyright in question, the court turned to access and substantial similarity. That there was access was not a question; substantial similarity was.

For the first time, the Ninth Circuit made explicit the "extrinsic" test for substantial similarities in the ideas and the "intrinsic" test for substantial similarities of the expression comprising two works. A finding of similarity of idea is ordinarily prerequisite to scrutiny for similarity in expression. Because the former depends on specific criteria subject to listing and analysis, it can be subjected to both analytical dissection and expert testimony. The extrinsic test is, in short, objective and can be decided as a matter of law. The intrinsic test, on the other hand, is more subtle and complex, depending on observation and impressions. It is subjective, and analysis is necessarily ad hoc. Idea and expression will rarely coincide. Coincidence occurs only where the expression provides nothing beyond the idea. In such a situation, protection would be afforded only where identical copying is shown. The scope of copyright protection, then, increases as expression expands upon the underlying idea.

Had the court in this case applied only the extrinsic test, the defendants' list of dissimilarities might well have represented an effective defense. But so analytical a dissection was held to be inappropriate. The proper intrinsic approach, addressing the impact of the works in question on the minds and imaginations of young people, revealed that the defendants had captured the total concept and "feel" of the plaintiffs' property. Such an analysis requires neither duplication nor near-identity in the competing materials. As a result, the intrinsic analysis is more sophisticated than the extrinsic.

Ultimately the Ninth Circuit held that "[t]he expression inherent in the H. R. Pufnstuf series differs markedly from its relatively simple idea. The characters... have developed personalities and particular ways of interacting with one another and their environment. The physical setting also has several unique features."[40] The matter had properly gone to the jury for an application of the test this circuit labelled intrinsic. And the verdict was not to be disturbed.

Above and beyond elucidation of the extrinsic and intrinsic approaches to similarity, the *Krofft* case stands for two major propositions of interest in considering copyright protection of fictional characters. First, idea and expression coincide only where the latter provides nothing beyond the former. Second, the scope of copyright protection expands as expression expands from idea.

A NOTE ON COPYRIGHT AND STATE COMMON LAW PROTECTION

Before proceeding to defenses to copyright infringement, it is important to relate federal statutory law to corresponding state law. Two U.S. Supreme Court cases address the situation in which the works in question are not protected by patent or copyright but could have been.[41] The works in question were lamps.

In the *Sears* case, the popular retailer was selling a pole lamp essentially identical to one designed and marketed by Stiffel, but at a much lower price. Plaintiff Stiffel was precluded from bringing a successful patent case and so brought a case based on unfair competition, alleging confusion to the public pursuant to Illinois case law. The lower courts had held in favor of Stiffel and enjoined Sears' activity. The Supreme Court, however, reversed on the theory that an unpatented item was in the public domain. To allow the state to apply its own law of unfair competition to prevent copying of an item the United States had ruled not entitled to protection was held to constitute a deprivation of the public of something that belongs to them by law. (The companion *Compco* case was resolved in comparable fashion.)

These cases show that, if a property is subject to federal patent or copyright law and has not been properly protected under the law, it *cannot* be protected under state law. Significantly, this is not the case pursuant to trademark law, because the states are allowed to regulate this component of unfair competition. The Congress has preempted only patent and copyright pursuant to constitutional protection of intellectual properties.

NOTES

1. Axelbank v. Rony, 277 F.2d 314 (9th Cir. 1960). For further discussion of history as a matter of public domain, *see* Hoehling v. Universal City Studios, 618 F.2d 972 (2d Cir. 1980).

2. 277 F.2d at 314. The libel action arose out of the plaintiff's letter accusing the defendant of being a pirate. This libel issue was resolved separately and has no bearing on the analysis of the infringement issues.

3. Miller v. Universal City Studios, 650 F.2d 1365 (5th Cir. 1981).

4. Harper & Row Publishers v. Nation Enterprises, 220 U.S.P.Q. 210 (S.D. N.Y. 1983).

5. 220 U.S.P.Q. at 213.

6. Wiren v. Shubert Theatre Corporation, 5 F. Supp. 358 (S.D. N.Y. 1933).

7. O'Neill v. Dell Publishing Co., 630 F.2d 683 (1st Cir. 1980).

8. *See* 17 U.S.C. 401–406, 411.

9. Smith v. Little, Brown & Company, 360 F.2d 928 (2d Cir. 1966).

10. Fenton McHugh Productions v. WGN Continental Productions, 216 U.S.P.Q. 173 (Ill. App. 1982).

11. Mann v. Columbia Pictures, 217 U.S.P.Q. 468 (Cal. App. 1982).

12. *See, e.g.*, Goodis v. United Artists Television, 425 F.2d 397 (2d Cir. 1970).

13. MacDonald v. Du Maurier, 144 F.2d 696 (2d Cir. 1944).

14. 144 F.2d at 701.

15. 155 F.2d at 702.

16. 144 F.2d at 702–703.

17. 144 F.2d at 703.

18. Mazer v. Stein, 347 U.S. 201, 74 S. Ct. 460 (1954).

19. Franklin Mint Corp. v. Nat. Wildlife Art Exchg., 575 F.2d 62 (3d Cir. 1978).

20. 575 F.2d at 65.

21. 575 F.2d at 65–66.

22.Arnstein v. Porter, 154 F.2d 464 (2d Cir. 1946).

23. W. STRONG, THE COPYRIGHT BOOK/A PRACTICAL GUIDE (2d ed. 1984), at 4–5.

24. Ibid., at 5.

25. Ibid., at 5–6.

26. Ibid., at 6–10.
27. Ibid., at 10. *See* note 29 *infra* and accompanying text.
28. M. MUNN, GREAT FILM EPICS/THE STORIES BEHIND THE SCENES (1982).
29. G. Ricordo & Co. v. Paramount Pictures, 189 F.2d 469 (2d Cir. 1951).
30. Sheldon v. Metro-Goldwyn-Mayer Pictures Corporation, 81 F.2d 49 (2d Cir. 1936), at 55–56.
31. Miller v. Columbia Broadcasting System, 209 U.S.P.Q. 502 (C.D. Cal. 1980).
32. Funkhouser v. Loew's Inc., 208 F.2d 185 (8th Cir. 1953).
33. Reyher v. Children's Television Workshop, 533 F.2d 87 (2d Cir. 1976).
34. 533 F.2d at 90.
35. Bradbury v. Columbia Broadcasting System, 287 F.2d 478 (9th Cir. 1961).
36. 287 F.2d at 484–485.
37. Universal City Studios v. Film Ventures Intern., 214 U.S.P.Q. 865 (C.D. Cal. 1982).
38. Bartsch v. Metro-Goldwyn-Mayer, 391 F.2d 150 (2d Cir. 1968).
39. Sid & Marty Krofft Television v. McDonald's Corp., 562 F.2d 1157 (9th Cir. 1977).
40. 562 F.2d at 1169. The Ninth Circuit also addressed in some detail the tension between copyright and First Amendment privilege, which is beyond the scope of this effort. *See* 562 F.2d at 1169–1171.
41. Sears Roebuck & Co. v. Stiffel Co., 84 S. Ct. 784, 376 U.S. 225, 11 L. Ed. 2d 661 (1964) and Compco Corp. v. Day-Brite Lighting, 84 S. Ct. 779, 376 U.S. 234, 11 L. Ed. 2d 669 (1964).

3

Copyright Protection in the Courts: Defenses to Copyright Infringement

MATERIAL IN THE PUBLIC DOMAIN

Assuming it cannot be shown that the allegedly infringing work actually derives from an independent source, the first line of defense to copyright infringement is a demonstration that the plaintiff's work is not subject to copyright. All such materials are said to be in the public domain. Besides being in the public domain ab initio, works once subject to copyright can lapse into the public domain by operation of law. This can prove to be a tricky situation, as illustrated when an individual sought to exploit a film version of *Pygmalion* some fifty years after George Bernard Shaw copyrighted the original dramatic work.[1]

Shaw had copyrighted *Pygmalion* in 1913. That copyright was renewed in 1941 and extended by Congress to 1988. In 1938 the derivative film *Pygmalion* was made under a licensing agreement with Shaw. Copyright in the film expired in 1966. Subsequently the proprietors of Shaw's original copyright licensed an exclusive distributor of the film, and still later the defendant rented it. The defendant argued with a certain appealing logic that the film was in the public domain and its prints could be freely exploited without infringement of the original copyright in Shaw's work. The court disagreed: "Although the derivative work may enter the public domain, the matter contained therein which derives from a work still covered by statutory copyright is not dedicated to the public."[2]

In the case of the films *Blue Lagoon* and *Paradise*, the result turned on what portions of the former were in fact new and original to it.[3] Since the novel *Blue Lagoon* was in the public domain, a successful action against *Paradise* depended on any distinctions from the underlying novel to be found in the *Blue Lagoon* film. Not until this starting point was established could the two films be subjected to scrutiny for substantial similarity.

Upon comparative analysis the court held that the general ideas of the two films (coming of age and the development of a relationship in *Blue Lagoon* in contrast to the chase of *Paradise*) were distinct and, further, that expression differed as well. For these and a variety of other reasons *Paradise* was held not to infringe *Blue Lagoon*.

THE MATTER OF SUBSTANTIAL SIMILARITY

Historical Perspective on the Law

As was the case in establishing an infringement action, the matter of substantial similarity frequently becomes the crux of the defense to claims of copyright infringement. Similarities in idea and in expression must both be addressed.

From the earliest cases and controversies courts have been faced with the tension between public access to different expressions of the same idea and the right of an author to preclude others from taking the expression comprising a specific treatment of that idea. The evolution of judicial approach to this crucial element of copyright assumes certain patterns in managing what is often a difficult question. Only in recent years have courts been willing to grant summary judgments dismissing actions through application of the extrinsic and intrinsic tests, applied respectively to idea and expression.

One early decision in the Second Circuit involved a comparison of the film operetta *I Dream Too Much* with the play *Depends on the Woman.*[4] The court engaged in a lengthy summary of the two works before concluding that the audience test, requiring the identity of expression be "capable of sensory perception by the audience," was inconclusive.[5]

The Second Circuit then engaged in a characteristic approach. First it stated the obvious: no copyright can exist where scenes are the common property of all playwrights. Then the court distinguished the theme of a work—its idea—from the plot—the sequence of events expressing that theme. The theme is not protectable. Moreover, in cases in which there are dissimilarities in character, locale, and action, as with the two works before the court, there can be no infringement.

Not many years later, the Southern District of New York engaged in essentially the same analysis in comparing the story, book, and film *My Man, Godfrey* with the play *This Modern Instance.*[6] Once again two developments of admittedly similar themes were held to be divergent. Moreover, the personalities of the two major characters were "as different as day and night" and lesser characters were dissimilar.[7] In short, based on a lengthy comparison, the differences in the two works were "radical and extreme."[8] Although neither of these New York courts used the phrase, a major concept behind their analytical approach is now known as *scènes à faire.*

Scènes à Faire

Shortly after the foregoing cases were decided, two articles were published. The first set out the ideals implicit to copyright law.[9] In reflecting on the affirmative protection of a work and the limitations on that protection, Zechariah Chafee observed that protection should never stifle the independent creation of others. While no one else may market another's work, the law does not go so far as to prohibit its use. Indeed, "[t]he world goes ahead because each of us builds on the work of our predecessors."[10]

The author expanded on this point to say:

> Even the first user of a plot or a human situation should not have a monopoly on it. The public should have the opportunity to see what

other artists will do with the same plot or situation. . . . Yet we want to encourage originality and not slavishness. There comes a point where the use of material is so close as not to give the public anything really new. At that point the ideal of encouraging independent creation ceases to operate.[11]

Unfortunately, it is no easy task to distinguish appropriation from creativity building on the past:

[T]he precise boundaries of . . . independent creation are hard to fix. Everybody agrees that the ideas in the copyrighted book are not protected. . . . [But] "expression" has too wide a range. . . . I like to say that the protection covers the "pattern" of the work.[12]

The second article addresses the matter of originality in the copyright context.[13] Here the opening observation is that the criterion of originality is not "newness of ideas" but "distinctive enfoldment."[14] Judge Leon R. Yankwich acknowledges that few dramatic situations are original. Instead "the history of literature indicates clearly what literary creativeness can do, not only with ordinary occurrences, but with incidents which are the common property of mankind."[15]

Yankwich goes on to say that in analyzing creative works for the presence of independent or different development, some legal precedent recognizes that when the common idea is treated, no matter how differently, common elements must emerge in the two works. To the extent that these elements are distinct, there is creative originality. In the course of analysis "the similarities which are traceable to the common sources are disregarded. But similarities may appear which are inherent in a situation. The French refer to them as *scènes à faire*,—that is, scenes which *must* follow a certain situation."[16] Even when character, locale, and action are similar, there is no infringement when they comprise scènes à faire, an extension of idea not rising to the level of expression.

In this context Yankwich considered characters and characterizations at some length.[17] Character *types* were equated with ideas. As such, the less developed a character (type), the less subject to copyright it will be. Conversely, logic dictates that the more developed an individual character, the greater the copyright protection is likely to be. This makes resolving issues of similarity more complex: "Important as characterizations are in novels and dramas, they present great difficulties. Throughout the ages, universal and distinctive characterizations have emerged from dramatic works."[18] How are distinctive new characters to be treated in court? English precedent holds that "unless, in addition to the characterization, incidents and situations of real substance, through which the character expresses itself, were also taken, there would be no actionable imitation."[19]

Melville B. Nimmer and David Nimmer offer an intensive survey of substantial similarity with specific reference to scènes à faire and characterizations.[20] They begin with the proposition that if the only similarity between two works is limited to a common "abstract" idea, substantial similarity is actually missing.[21] They accept the dichotomy between idea and expression and note the judicial tests employed to make the distinction between the two and effect their subsequent analysis.[22] In reviewing the "pattern" test propounded by Learned Hand of the Second Circuit, the authors compare *West Side Story* to *Romeo and Juliet*. Using this test, thirteen basic similarities are found. The crucial similarities move from the membership of the boy and girl in hostile groups through their meeting at a dance to the boy's suicide upon his erroneous belief in the girl's death. The conclusion is that substantial similarity is indeed reflected in the extensive pattern of similarities.[23] But this is a matter of plot. There are courts that have held plot to be no more than an abstract idea and thus unprotectable.[24] Nimmer and Nimmer include in the concept of scènes à faire not only incidents or plot necessarily following from a common theme or setting but also any similarity of expression necessarily resulting "from the fact that the common idea is only capable of expression in more or less stereotyped form".[25]

The case law. Commentary may be instructive—even provocative, but significant developments can proceed only through judicial opinion. The concept of scènes à faire often arises in defense of infringement actions. In fact, it is a defense that frequently results in summary judgment for defendants.

In recent cases, courts of the Second and Ninth Circuits have taken nearly identical stands in measuring substantial similarity by this yardstick. In comparing the novel *Roots* to the novel *Jubilee* and a related pamphlet, the Southern District of New York first held that folklore and custom are not subject to copyright protection.[26] Then the court reiterated that no one writes a book of purely original intent. Thereupon the court entered into the matter of scènes à faire. In the context of these works, the following pattern was dismissed as scènes à faire: attempted escapes, flights through woods pursued by baying dogs, sorrowful or happy singing by slaves, the buying and selling of human beings, and other miseries of slavery in America. The defense was granted its motion for summary judgment.

Only a few years later, this district once again addressed scènes à faire with the same result.[27] This time the film *Stir Crazy* was being compared to a series of comedies involving imprisoned black and white protagonists who escape through the device of a prison rodeo. With regard to scènes à faire, the court accepted as a protectable development the rodeo as an escape vehicle. But it limited that protection to those points where this general theme is particularized into characters, details, and events.

The court held that the works were dissimilar in particularization. It found the similarities at this level to be insignificant and the dissimilarities significant. There were five principle similarities:

1. The rodeo device, motivating and dictating the manner of escape
2. An inexperienced city boy who comes between the warden and the top hand, thus gaining favor
3. The role of the city boy in upsetting the warden's plans
4. Characters of the protagonists and their roles in the rodeo
5. A mass murderer who terrifies others but befriends the protagonists

This district also held that the plaintiff had failed to establish substantial similarity in character portrayals. Specifically, a "city boy," a "top hand," and a black protagonist (even when played by the same actor, Richard Pryor), are all characterizations too general to deserve protection.[28]

Characterization was again considered in the context of scènes à faire when a New York district court was called upon to compare *Raiders of the Lost Ark* to the screenplay *Black Rainbow*.[29] Although copyright and access were expressly conceded, the mood and feel of the two works were found to be entirely different. Here the defense of scènes à faire was of little significance. That defense merely attached to certain similarities occurring in comparable scenes and dialogue that were insignificant. The court focused its attention on the respective elaborations of plot, settings, and characters in the two works.

The settings were dissimilar—South America and Cairo in contrast to the Peruvian jungle. The plot of *Black Rainbow* was dismissed as a "sombre, vulgar script replete with overt sexual scenes, cocaine smuggling and cold-blooded killing" while *Raiders* was hailed as a "tongue-in-cheek, action packed, . . . all-American adventure."[30]

Most significantly, the characters reflected no substantial similarity, even though both protagonists were male archaeologists. One was a serious, self-interested traitor and killer while the other was a "larger-than-life adventurer who, in the matinee-idol fashion, remains loyal to truth, justice and the American way."[31] The two principal villains were also found to be dissimilar, as were the respective heroines, who shared nothing more in common than their gender and sexual encounters with the respective heroes.

In another case involving a comparison of the novel and film *Coming Home* to their alleged source, the Southern District of New York found irrelevant testimony to the effect that there were striking parallels in plot, theme, mood, time, character development, setting, and pace.[32] Upon a close reading of the novel and a critical viewing of the film, the court essentially found that rather imposing array of similarities to be scènes à faire. Both works considered the effects of the Vietnam War on the lives of individuals through a love triangle, of which the betrayed member commits suicide. The court observed that "the essence of infringement lies in taking not a general theme but its particular expression through similarities of treatment, details, scenes, events and characters."[33]

Not surprisingly, the Second Circuit has engaged in comparable analyses.[34] The court's opinion in *Reyher v. Children's Television Workshop* neatly sums up the judicial approach, in what is now standard language.

Based on the special relationship between parent and child, both works present the thematic concept that to a lost child, the familiar face of the mother is the most beautiful face, even though the mother is not, in fact, beautiful to most. The overlapping sequences of events concern the lost child finding his or her mother, albeit with some difficulty because of the description given. This similarity of events, however, may be considered *scènes à faire*, scenes which necessarily result from identical situations. Thus, where a lost child is the protagonist, there is likely to be a reunion with parents. Furthermore, the morals stated by the two stories differ in emphasis. Reyher's book focuses on how love makes people appear beautiful, while the CTW story stresses that what is beautiful to some may not be beautiful to others. More importantly, however, the two works differ in "total feel." ... The two stories are not similar in mood, details or characterization.[35]

At issue in the *Hoehling* case were accounts of the Hindenburg disaster, both factual and fictional. The plaintiff had thoroughly researched the event in preparing the book *Who Destroyed the Hindenburg?* The first half of that work covered the crossing from Europe to America, the second the subsequent investigations. After discarding alternative explanations for the disaster, the plaintiff concluded with an identification of the alleged saboteur, based on the presence of motive, expertise, and opportunity.

The defendant's film about the Hindenburg followed the formula, identified with *Grand Hotel*, common to contemporaneous "disaster" films. The film was drawn from a fictional account, which itself had drawn on the plaintiff's materials in addition to original files on the disaster.

The Second Circuit acknowledged the virtual impossibility of writing about any historical era or fictional theme without the use of certain stock literary devices that have been identified as scènes à faire, uncopyrightable as a matter of law. The problem to be addressed, according to the court, was the point of demarcation between scènes à faire and protected expression.

The court declined to begin with an elimination of similarities based on noncopyrightable elements, noting that wholesale usurpation of a prior work's expression might thus be overlooked. Instead it asserted the necessity for deciding whether the alleged infringement is virtually identical to its predecessor. Where the subject matter is historical, the analysis will be fairly liberal.

The plaintiff here claimed that the defendants had copied essential elements of plot, notably including destruction by a saboteur. The Second Circuit disagreed, finding independent interpretations of historical fact. The plaintiff's remaining allegations of similarity were also dismissed as no more than "random duplications of phrases and sequences of events,"—scènes à faire, identified with " 'incidents, characters or settings which are as a practical matter indispensable, or at least standard, in the treatment of a given topic.' "[36]

In comparing the film *Trading Places* with the screenplay *High Stakes*, a California district court dismissed copyright infringement with prejudice, deciding that the ideas were not substantially similar and, as a matter of law, that the expression was dissimilar.[37] The basic themes and premises were held to be dissimilar as were the mood and pace as well as the plot and sequence of events, even though both works involved major transformation in a principal character. Certain similarities were dismissed as random and insignificant, without pertinence to the total concept and feel of the two works. Other similarities were held to be unprotectable as scènes à faire. The standard judicial language was repeated with regard to incidents, characters, and settings.

The Ninth Circuit has held accordingly in making comparisons between works of science fiction, including *E.T.—The Extraterrestrial* and *Lokey from Maldemar*[38] and *Coma* and *Reincarnation, Inc.*[39] In the E.T. case, the Ninth Circuit disapproved lengthy lists of similarities as a point of departure, finding such lists inherently subjective and unreliable, especially when the items are scattered throughout the works in question. The court did concede that certain opening scenes in the two works went beyond stock treatment but found no similarity in sequence, mood, dialogue, or characters beyond a generalized, unprotected level.

The court found major distinctions with regard to the characters. Then it made a telling observation: "As is too often the case, [plaintiff's] action was premised 'partly upon a wholly erroneous understanding of the extent of copyright protection; and partly upon that obsessive conviction, so common among authors . . . that all similarities between their works and any others which appear later must inevitably be ascribed to plagiarism.' "[40]

In deciding the *Coma* case, this circuit found the works to be dissimilar upon application of both the extrinsic and intrinsic tests. Then it repeated the basic reasoning: "It is well established that, as a matter of law, certain forms of literary expression are not protected against copying. . . . [T]he general idea for a story is among these. So too are all situations and incidents which flow naturally from a basic plot premise, so-called scenes a faire."[41]

The Northern District of Illinois has engaged in comparable analyses of the science fiction films, *Starman* and *Wavelength*.[42] The plaintiff had identified similarities in the characters, setting, and action. Here again the comparison was divided between elements of characterization and of matters comprising scènes à faire.

The similarities between these films, described as "indispensable elements to the treatment of this type of science fiction theme,"[43] consisted of

1. An alien trying to return home (a long-standing plot)
2. Pursuit by the government
3. Rescue by friendly humans
4. General human fear of the alien
5. Return home just before death

The Ninth Circuit found crucial distinctions between the characters in the two works. The alien characters were portrayed differently in terms of age, numbers, communication and relationships with human protagonists, and attitudes toward humanity.

FAIR USE AND PARODY

Fair Use

There are cases in which both access and substantial similarity are conceded. Then two additional defenses regarding the matter of protection afforded characters are brought to bear. These defenses are fair use and its special offspring, parody.

Fair use has been described as a rule of reason balancing an author's right to compensation against the public's interest in the widest possible dissemination of ideas and information.[44] Fair use, in essence, admits to a certain basic similarity. In fact it is often a matter of direct copying or, as in the case of parody, a recognizable taking with an alteration in feel and concept.

Perhaps the best illustration of what is—and is not—fair use of popular properties involves the character Pac-Man.[45] At issue was the book, *How To Win at Pac-Man.* The pictures and text were held to be fair use but the use of Pac-Man characters on the cover was found to be promotional—not fair use. The highly pragmatic court reasoned that it is the merit of the comment, criticism, or review that should sell a book. Such is the basis of the fair use defense—allowing comment, criticism, and review, not merely in the name of political freedom, but also for societal welfare and the improvement of specific enterprises. None of these uses, however, justifies the appropriation of a copyright for strictly marketing purposes. Recognition of appropriation in a marketing context was attributed to Congress in the provision distinguishing uses of a commercial nature from nonprofit educational purposes.[46] The latter is more likely to be held fair use.

With continued pragmatism the court enjoined future publication of the book with the infringing cover but ordered no recall of books already in circulation.

Parody

The form of fair use known as parody may serve to clarify any ambiguity associated with fair use. There are two leading cases in point. In one, the similarities were too close and parody was not acceptable as a defense.[47] In the second, parody was a defense to the infringement action.[48] The two are companion cases in California's Southern District.

The first case involved the film *Gaslight*, an intense psychological melodrama in which Charles Boyer portrays an evil husband attempting to drive his rather naive wife, played by Ingrid Bergman, to madness. She is saved at the last moment by the hero, played by Joseph Cotton. The film was extremely successful and in rerelease when Jack Benny broadcast a parody of it for radio and then television.

On radio Jack Benny took on the Charles Boyer role, and Ingrid Bergman performed a travesty on her own role. Significantly, the Benny production did secure permission to air the parody for radio. The problem arose with the subsequent television broadcast starring Barbara Stanwyck. The plaintiff objected by letter, and the defendant responded citing fair use. When a longer version of the parody was performed, the plaintiff filed suit. It was the longer version that was enjoined.

The court began with the observation that fair use would be given broader scope when the context of litigation is the field of education. The scope is to be considerably reduced in takings solely for commercial gain. It then acknowledged that television is in active competition with motion pictures.

The court analyzed the two works in some detail and found that Benny utilized a variety of comic devices in the public domain to invert the mood from tragic to humorous. Yet tragedy and comedy were compared to love and hate, both pairs representing opposite faces of the same coin. The case tested the proposition that no case can be found allowing as fair use the wholesale copying of copyrighted material.[49] At that point, the court observed that under the law the taker or user of another's property (including intellectual property) acts at his own peril.[50]

The companion case analyzed Sid Caesar's answer to *From Here to Eternity—From Here to Obscurity*. This time the California district observed the difficulty it was facing in trying to determine just how far television could go in taking from the cinema with a reference to the *Gaslight* case. Where, it asked, is the line to be drawn in each individual case?[51]

The court then proceeded to set out six principles to be applied in drawing that fine line separating infringement from fair use:

1. Burlesque is not per se a defense.
2. Some limited taking should be permitted because the intent of burlesque is to conjure up at least a general image of the original.
3. Burlesque may take scènes à faire.
4. Burlesque may take beyond scènes à faire so long as the taking is not substantial.
5. Such expanded taking is a calculated risk, subject to review by the trier of fact.
6. Where the same character is involved, the line is more strictly drawn than otherwise.

In deciding that *From Here to Obscurity* was a case of fair use, the court also announced the test to be applied on the basis of the six principles. The test is more qualitative than quantitative, calling for a new, original and different development, treatment, and expression. No substantial similarity was found between the two works in terms of theme, characterizations, story line, sequence, dialogue, points of suspense, subclimax, or climax.[52] In other words, *From Here to Obscurity* did not cross the line beyond recalling and conjuring up *From Here to Eternity*; it did not trespass into substantial similarity.

A recent attempt to parody *Gone with the Wind* did cross the line.[53] The defendant's property, *Scarlett Fever*, was found to be a synopsis of the original with songs and dance routines inserted cabaret style. The settings included Tiara and Thirteen Elms. Among the defendant's characters were Shady Charlotte O'Mara, Brett Studler, Melody Hampton, and Ansley Mall.

Scarlett Fever was held to fall short of fair use and thus was primarily derivative. Even to the extent the court accepted the presence of parody, the production was too close to the original.

The court obviously found the effort to be more nearly a musical version of *Gone with the Wind*. While the court accepted parody as a prerequisite to the issue of fair use, it found no critical comment or statement to provide any social value beyond simple entertainment.

The court then examined the elements of the production and engaged in some rather astute distinctions, illustrating basic principles of infringement. The songs were found to be both noninfringing and protected. Satire was found in the treatment of Melanie/Melody and of some of the other characters, as well as in the name of the play. However, other characters, notably Charlotte/Scarlett, were simply comic exaggerations, and Brett/Rhett was played straight. More to the point, the court found that *Scarlett Fever*, by reason of its very popularity, was likely to damage the potential of any future stage production of *Gone with the Wind*.

Two decisions against *Scarlett Fever* did not end the matter. The defendants went on to argue that the plaintiffs had abandoned their rights, notably in not acting against Carol Burnett's television treatment of *Gone with the Wind*. The court noted first that there was no such thing as a limited abandonment as suggested by the defendants and second that the Burnett treatment (retelling the entire story in ten minutes) was a parody. In fact, the plaintiffs had never given approval to any spoof.

The Second Circuit has found parody in affirming a summary judgment favoring *Mad Magazine*'s satiric renditions of the lyrics of popular songs, including "The First Time I Saw (Roger) Maris" sung to "The Last Time I Saw Paris" and "Louella Schwartz Describes Her Malady" sung to "A Pretty Girl Is Like a Melody."[54] That circuit observed that for the most part, the rhyme scheme of the parodies bore no relationship whatsoever to that of the originals, although brief phrases of the original lyrics were injected as necessary to recall the originals. The humorous effect was achieved when a familiar line was interposed in a totally incongruous setting, a traditional tool of parody, hardly amounting to a substantial taking. Similarly, the fact that the defendant's parodies were written in the same meter as the plaintiff's compositions was held inevitable for recognition of the original. In any event the Second Circuit doubted that even Irving Berlin should be permitted to claim a property right in iambic pentameter.[55]

Less innocent parodies of Walt Disney characters have not been so successful.[56] The pornographic depictions of Disney characters by defendant were infringements. Rhyming packages spoofing Tetley tea ("Tetley Tea Bags/Petley Flea Bags, Tiny Little Dog Fleas"), on the other hand, were amenable to this defense.[57] Some years ago McDonald's ran an advertisement spoofing *Jaws*. Visually and musically the commercial for the Whaler sandwich was a parody of commercials for the film. Apparently no law suit ever resulted.

CASE IN POINT: *STAR WARS v. BATTLESTAR GALACTICA*

It is plaintiffs who ordinarily establish the legal battleground. In the comparison of *Star Wars* to *Battlestar Galactica*, no character, aspect, or individual sequence was isolated: one film as a whole was compared to another film as a whole.[58]

Similarity of ideas, the extrinsic test. The initial step was comparison of the ideas underlying the two creations. The California district found the ideas underlying *Star Wars* and *Battlestar Galactica* different as a matter of law. Even though both films involve a struggle between good and evil in space, they do differ substantially as to story line, central characters, and many other aspects.[59] In contrast to *Star Wars*, *Battlestar Galactica* was neither pure fantasy nor a morality play. It was a simplistic good-guys-versus-bad-guys story with a large dose of sex and temptation, twentieth-century television style. Its altogether *human* characters, with all their weaknesses and feelings, are placed in situations all can relate to—except that those familiar scenes all take place in a space setting.

What proceeds from that start is ubiquitous on television: in the Civil War stories, in the stories of the two world wars, in some of the stories of the sodbusters versus the cattlemen, and so on. In short, according to the California district, *Battlestar Galactica* could just as well be the cowboys versus the Indians, except for the setting. Significantly, all the characters, including all those who are central to the action, are quite human with weaknesses and feelings that are very familiar.[60]

Similarities of expression, the intrinsic test. The court could have stopped with this initial finding. But, instead, it proceeded to the expression of the ideas in the two creative products in an effort to avoid remand upon an appellate finding that those basic ideas were similar. Expression was reviewed in the context of plot, language (centering on the word droid) and characters.

Language similarities were held to be insignificant. Expression of the plot was found not to be substantially similar. The total concept and feel of the two films was held to be vastly different. In referring to the *Krofft* case (chapter 2) the court noted that the two films are far more complex: In the first instance, each runs for more than two hours.

More to the point, each portrays a number of main characters and dozens of secondary characters, developed at least to some extent. Each tells a complex story. The court found it nearly impossible to reduce such complex works to a single idea. To do so would require a description so general as to be almost meaningless.[61]

While *Battlestar Galactica* was described as a simplistic recasting of a story out of a series of popular genres, *Star Wars* was seen as pure fantasy, a morality play. The plaintiffs themselves contended that the film's power follows from the fact that it is a mythical work recalling classic morality plays. Evidence revealed its strength to lie in the audience's identification with the mythic aspects of the story. To describe *Star Wars* as a morality play captures its essence as a whole.[62]

On the other hand, the evil forces against whom the good people of *Battlestar Galactica* strive are all robots, except for one human traitor. Major elements in *Battlestar Galactica* are the unrest among the people on the spaceships, their distrust of their leader, and the leaders' struggle to maintain control of them. Another is the people's yielding to temptation when they finally reach an oasis.

Their story is a restatement, in futuristic dress, of the Israelites going through the desert and reveling in their camp while Moses is on Mt. Sinai. None of these essential elements of *Galactica* is found in *Star Wars*.

Because the two works were subject to overall comparison, the court was not inclined to consider individual elements. It did, however, turn its attention to three benchmark similarities selected by the plaintiffs: the *X*-shaped fighters, the mask of Darth Vader and of the Cylons, and the cantina sequences. All were summarily rejected as in the public domain.

The cantina scenes received the most consideration. First, the cantina scenes were placed in the context of other such scenes in films such as *Casablanca* and *Caberet*. With sly understatement the court acknowledged that the cantina scenes in the two works did include some unusual types. But the two were not comparable. There was no similarity between the highly imaginative and fanciful cantina scene in *Star Wars*, in which nearly all the patrons were nonhuman, and the more commonplace scene of human revelry in *Battlestar Galactica*.[63] The works were found to be substantially different in plot, concept, and feel and in delineation and description of their central characters. The relationship of those characters to each other also differed.[64] Central to the *Star Wars* plot is Luke Skywalker. The film shows his maturation, his coming of age. He is the basic rural youth, following peaceful pursuits while searching for self-identity, who becomes involved in battle as a major warrior. *Battlestar Galactica* has no such single clearly central character but focuses on a father and son who are a leader and a professional fighter. Unlike Luke Skywalker, the son is introduced as an adult with an established identity.

The court described the characters of *Star Wars* with considerable insight: Luke Skywalker was described as flawless, both greater and purer than life. Princess Leia was described as untouchable and unreal, also purer than life—more symbol than actual person.

Obi-Wan Kenobi was equated with God, the touchstone of morality and the giver of the essential philosophy of life. In short, he, too, is unreal and symbolic. Darth Vader is similarly unreal and symbolic. He is Mephistopheles, the incarnation of evil.

The only character in *Star Wars* that the court attributed with mundane human traits and feelings was Han Solo, described as both less important and less central than the others. Han Solo is a stereotypical sidekick.[65]

The result. In concluding the lack of similarity as a matter of law and thus granting the defendants their summary dismissal, this district court observed that it is immaterial that multiple elements of superficial similarity can be isolated. As long as the expression of the idea is different and there is no substantial similarity of the works taken as a whole, there can be no infringement.[66]

The court went so far as to address the defendants' motives with reference to the immense, unprecedented success of *Star Wars*. Admittedly, there was evidence that the defendants were attempting to capitalize on the renewed interest in space fantasy produced by *Star Wars*. A working title of their initial effort, developed shortly after the release of *Star Wars*, was "Star World."[67] This, however, is a matter whose remedy is not legal but in the hands of critics and the fans.

The court aptly concluded that no one owns the genre of space fantasy or of space warfare. Legally, imitators are allowed to try to claim a share of the market and to seek some benefit from the public interest in the genre so long as they avoid substantial similarity with a predecessor protected by copyright.[68]

Result on Appeal

For all the district court's astute analysis, this decision was in fact reversed and remanded.[69] With both copyright and access conceded, the Ninth Circuit reviewed a videotape montage of science fiction, viewed *Star Wars*, and read the novelization and viewed the first episode of *Battlestar Galactica*. That viewing raised a genuine issue of material fact. According to the circuit court, reasonable minds could differ on the matter of similarities in idea and expression. Indeed it perceived some thirty-four similarities, of which it listed thirteen, including:

1. The central conflict in a war between the galaxy s democratic and totalitarian forces

2. The hero's father figure
3. Leadership of a wise old man with mystical qualities
4. The hero's return home to find it destroyed
5. Friendly robots
6. Conclusion with an awards ceremony honoring the heroes

Postscript

In literature and law as elsewhere, turnabout is fair play: as reported in an article in *Cinefantastique*, an artist filed suit against the *Star Wars* team for lifting his designs. The artist claimed that the bipedal walkers, reminiscent of oversized chickens, of *The Empire Strikes Back*, were misappropriated from his "sprinters." The designs had been sold in the midseventies at West Coast science fiction and comic book conventions. Working models, suitable for stop-motion cinematography, could be built from blueprints.[70]

The article does not indicate what theory was advanced: copyright or trademark infringement. In any event the judge ruled the suit to be a hoax during the pretrial interval. The plaintiff could produce no evidence of his assertions. As a matter of fact, he could not even produce the drawings at issue.[71]

These articles illustrate the fact that many cases revolving around aspects of popular literary properties are not necessarily resolved in court. They are not, however, lost on those in the relevant businesses. For example, Roger Corman in 1960 commissioned a film script. Years later a theatrical producer discovered the film to be in the public domain because of a legal technicality. The story and the characters were developed into a hit musical, *Little Shop of Horrors*. When Steven Spielberg and a colleague acquired the rights to produce a big-budget film adaptation of the musical, they encountered difficulties with the originators of the earlier film. This situation was resolved out of court in a settlement addressing both money and screen credits. The matter will be found in no court report but did appear in a film magazine.[72]

INFRINGEMENT DEFENSE AND CHARACTERS

While none of the cases in this chapter actually turns on characterization or copyright in characters, they do set the stage for copyright property in characters themselves. Assuming a work protected by copyright, access to that work, and the absence of an external source; character infringement—to the extent it exists in the copyright context—must turn on substantial similarity. In accord with existing precedent, the character at issue must rise above mere idea and be developed beyond the scope encompassed in scènes à faire. How this analysis is conducted will depend on each jurisdiction's placement of character among literary elements.

The question is a difficult one. Characters, along with location and action, may not rise above a scènes à faire extension of idea. At the other extreme they may *be* actionable expression.

NOTES

1. Russell v. Price, 612 F.2d 1123 (9th Cir. 1979).
2. 612 F.2d at 1128.
3. Columbia Pictures Industries v. Embassy Pictures, 218 U.S.P.Q. 497 (C.D. Cal. 1982).
4. Shipman v. R.K.O. Radio Pictures, 100 F.2d 533 (2d Cir. 1938).
5. 100 F.2d at 536.
6. West v. Hatch, 49 F. Supp. 307 (S.D. N.Y. 1943).
7. 49 F. Supp. at 312.
8. 49 F. Supp. at 308, 309–312.
9. Chafee, *Reflections on the Law of Copyright: I*, 45 COLUM. L. REV. 503 (1945), at 504–515.
10. Ibid., at 511.
11. Ibid., at 514.
12. Ibid., at 513.
13. Yankwich, *Originality in the Law of Intellectual Property (Its Meaning from a Legal and Literary Standpoint)*, 11 F.R.D. 457 (1952).
14. Ibid., at 458.
15. Ibid., at 472.
16. Ibid., at 462.
17. Ibid., at 465–472.
18. Ibid., at 466.
19. Ibid.

20. 3M. NIMMER AND D. NIMMER, NIMMER ON COPYRIGHT §13.03[A] (1988) at 13–20—13–62, §13.03[A][1] (1988) at 13–23, 13–31—13–34.
21. Ibid., §13.03[A][1] at 13–22.
22. Ibid., at 13–22.2—13–35.
23. Ibid., at 13–26—13–27.
24. Ibid., at 13–28—13–29.
25. Ibid., at 13–33.
26. Alexander v. Haley, 460 F. Supp. 40 (S.D. N.Y. 1978).
27. Smith v. Weinstein, 578 F. Supp. 1297 (S.D. N.Y. 1984).
28. 578 F. Supp. at 1303.
29. Zambito v. Paramount Pictures Corp., 613 F. Supp. 1107 (C.D. N.Y. 1985).
30. 613 F. Supp. at 1111.
31. Ibid.
32. Davis v. United Artists, 547 F. Supp. 722 (S.D. N.Y. 1982).
33. 547 F. Supp. at 726. (Footnote omitted.)
34. Reyher v. Children's Television Workshop, 533 F.2d 87 (2d Cir. 1976), *cert. den.* 429 U.S. 87, 97 S. Ct. 492, 50 L. Ed. 588 (1976).
35. 533 F.2d at 92. (Footnotes omitted.)
36. Hoehling v. Universal City Studios, 618 F.2d 972 (2d Cir. 1980), at 979.
37. Anderson v. Paramount Pictures Corp., 617 F. Supp. (C.D. Cal. 1985).
38. Litchfield v. Spielberg, 736 F.2d 1352 (9th Cir. 1984).
39. Berkic v. Crichton, 761 F.2d 1289 (9th Cir. 1985).
40. 736 F.2d at 1358.
41. 761 F.2d at 1293.
42. Wavelength Film v. Columbia Pictures, 631 F. Supp. 305 (N.D. Ill. 1986).
43. 631 F.2d at 307.
44. Triangle Publications v. Knight-Ridder Newspapers, 626 F.2d 1171 (C.D. Cal. 1982).

Fair use in the sense of direct copying for use in the classroom or elsewhere will not be addressed here.

45. PAC-MAN, 24 Pat. Trademark & Copyright (BNA) 5111 (September 23, 1982), reporting Publications Int'l. v. Bally Mfg. Corp., decided by the U.S. District Court for the Northern District of Illinois on July 14, 1982).
46. Ibid., at 5112.
47. Loew's Incorporated v. Columbia Broadcasting System, 131 F. Supp. 165 (S.D. Cal. 1955).
48. Columbia Pictures Corp. v. National Broadcasting Co., 137 F. Supp. 348 (S.D. Cal. 1955).

49. 131 F. Supp. at 183.
50. Ibid.
51. 137 F. Supp. at 350.
52. 137 F. Supp. at 352.
53. Metro-Goldwyn-Mayer v. Showcase Atlanta Co-op Prod., 479 F. Supp. 351. (N.D. GA. 1981).
54. Berlin v. E.C. Publications, 329 F.2d 541 (2d Cir. 1964).
55. 329 F.2d at 545.
56. *See* Walt Disney Productions v. Air Pirates, 581 F. 2d 751 (9th Cir. 1978).
57. Tetley v. Topps Chewing Gum, 556 F. Supp. 785 (E.D. NY. 1983).
58. Twentieth Century-Fox Film Corp. v. MCA, 209 U.S.P.Q. 200 (C.D. Cal. 1980). Note that, although a theatrical version of *Battlestar Galactica* was released and, presumably, competed directly with *Star Wars*, plaintiffs were acting against the television series as well. Presumably, the series (in trademark terms) represented a dilution of *Star Wars* properties.
59. 209 U.S.P.Q. at 203.
60. 209 U.S.P.Q. at 204.
61. 209 U.S.P.Q. at 204.
62. 209 U.S.P.Q. at 202.
63. 209 U.S.P.Q. at 204.
64. 209 U.S.P.Q. at 206.
65. 209 U.S.P.Q. at 204.
66. 209 U.S.P.Q. at 205.
67. 209 U.S.P.Q. at 207.
68. 209 U.S.P.Q. at 207–208.
69. Twentieth Century-Fox Film Corp. v. MCA, 715 F.2d 1327 (9th Cir. 1983).
70. Clarke, *Battle of the Walkers*, 14 CINEFANTASTIQUE 11 (1984).
71. *Lucasfilm Lawsuit: Judge Rules a Hoax*, 15 CINEFANTASTIQUE 13 (1985).

The articles cited here and in the preceding note illustrate the fact that many cases revolving around aspects of popular literary properties are not necessarily resolved in court.

72. Fisher, *Little Shop of Horrors/Corman's Now-Classic B-Film Ends up on Stage—and in Court*, 14 CINEFANTASTIQUE (1983/1984), at 12.

4

Trademark Protection and Unfair Competition

BASIC PRINCIPLES OF TRADEMARK ACTIONS

It is essential to review early trademark cases for the basic principles before considering the application of this property to literary works, dramatizations, and, most particularly, fictional characters. The intellectual property known as trademark is protected pursuant to federal statute and through the laws of the several states.[1] The violation of trademark rights is a form of unfair competition, which may be sanctioned through either codified or case law in the federal or state courts.

In a sense complementary to copyright in affected properties, trademark protects one or more names, to some extent dissociated from content or expression. Trademark is a unique manifestation of the source of a product—for the purposes of this work some component of literary property. If the trademarked name is not unique, it must have acquired secondary meaning among the consuming public in order for the necessary association with a specific source to attach. Otherwise the name is in general usage, or generic.

In addition to outright misappropriation of a mark ("palming" or "passing off" or merely instilling "confusion" among consumers), proprietors are often faced with its "dilution," referring to acts that somehow reduce the value of a trademark. Each form of illicit appropriation constitutes unfair competition. Unlike copyright, trademark is of potentially unlimited duration, but the latter is more vulnerable to devolution into public property than is the former. This devolution renders a trademark generic, no longer entitled to protection. It has been constructively abandoned, notwithstanding any effort on the part of the proprietor to preserve the exclusive property.

For purposes of protecting fictional characters, early trademark cases can demonstrate how widespread popularity can work against the object of public adulation. In the legal sense, the public can literally make a property its own. The fans of a character can actually usurp that character to deprive the original author of control. Here, issues of inadvertent abandonment and dilution take the place of substantial similarity as the center of judicial reasoning.

The familiar terms *aspirin* and *cellophane* illustrate the difficulties a proprietor can have in preserving trademark rights. Both terms were once trademarks that entered the public domain to become generic through public usage Today the propensity for such loss of trademark is implicit in the major effort to preserve Xerox as a trademark for xerographic copying, one prominent example among many in the marketplace.

Inadvertent Loss of Trademark

Before 1921 Aspirin was a trademark. The Bayer Company registered Aspirin as a trademark in the United States in 1899. For whatever reason the company chose not to appeal the 1918 cancellation of registration. Not much later, however, Bayer filed suit to enjoin the infringement of the trademark (on the basis of its common law status), charging unfair competition.[2] The defense was that the patent had expired on the drug and it was therefore in the public domain. Further, *aspirin* described the drug—that was the drug's name.

The question the Court of Appeals for the Second Circuit asked (through Justice Learned Hand) was what the buyers understood by the use of the word at issue, the crucial point being "if they understood by it only the kind of goods sold, then . . . it makes no difference whatever what efforts plaintiff has made to get them to understand more."[3] For the answer the court did not look to the class of buyers to whom Bayer was selling directly: manufacturing chemists, physicians, and perhaps retail druggists. The court instead looked to the general consuming public. This public knew aspirin as a type of drug, rather than as an indication of its source. The public understanding, then, determines whether a name or other symbol is a trademark, that is, indicative of source, or nothing more than a description of the goods.

DuPont faced a similar problem with its Cellophane.[4] In this case the defendant was selling cellulose sheets in response to requests for cellophane. There was no proof that any of the defendant's buyers thought they were obtaining DuPont's product. The trial court had held that the defendant either had to stop using the word *cellophane* or stop selling the material without an explanation.

The Second Circuit took a closer look at the circumstances and modified the result. As a preliminary matter, the circuit court agreed that no voluntary abandonment had occurred. Once again the crucial factor was public understanding. The question here was whether the word at issue simply meant "a transparent glycerinated cellulose hydrate regenerated from viscose, and nothing more, or . . . such an article of commerce manufactured by or originating with the complainant".[5]

According to the court, both the original inventor and DuPont were treating the term as generic. Customers, then, were seeking a satisfactory commodity rather than the product of a specific firm. In fact, retail dealers were unaware of another name to call the particular article. In short *cellophane* was found to be a descriptive word in general use. Thus, since "[t]he rights of the complainant must be based upon a wrong which the defendant has done to it by misleading customers as to the origin of the goods and thus taking away its trade" and since "[s]uch rights are not founded on a bare title to a word or symbol but on a cause of action to prevent deception", DuPont did not prevail on appeal.[6] Nevertheless, in modifying the lower court's order, the appellate court noted that each vendor of cellophane should be named, e.g., DuPont's or Sylvania's cellophane.

Xerox is currently going to great lengths to avoid inadvertent abandonment of its trademark. For example, in advertisements appearing in 1983, Xerox published what appears to be the entry for *duplicate* in *Roget's Thesaurus*. The word *Xerox*, found among the nouns and verbs, is circled in red and the headline reads "You can't always take Roget's word for it." The copy goes on to state that Xerox is neither a noun nor a verb but a proper adjective always to be followed by a verb or phrase describing a product of Xerox Corporation. Unfortunately for holders of trademarks, however, the public declines to be controlled in such matters. It will be interesting to see if Xerox ever does become xerox.

Retention of Trademark

In a recent successful effort to protect a trademark in ladies' "hair-retaining" combs, the Second Circuit provided some clarifying language.[7] The plaintiff's trademark was Feathercomb, a name held to be both widely known to the public and associated with the producer. The defendant was using the name Featherlight. In a basic affirmation of the district court's permanent injunction against the defendant, the appellate court offered the following observations:

1. A valid trademark must serve as an indication of origin.
2. It is not necessary that purchasers actually know the name of the manufacturer or producer.
3. It is sufficient that the public normally assumes that articles bearing the same mark are from the same source.
4. When the mark no longer indicates origin and merely informs of the nature or class of an article, the holder of the mark "suffers a total loss of rights in it."[8] (The mark becomes generic.)
5. In this case defendant Solo had every right to market a comb similar to or even identical to that marketed by its competitor. But if Solo did so, the law clearly imposed the obligation to promote its product so as not to be unduly confusing to the average consumer.[9]

In a most interesting case decided in the same era, the U.S. Supreme Court actually allowed the defendant to use the plaintiff's trademarked product in its own product.[10] The defendant was purchasing plaintiff Coty's toilet powder and perfumes. After a certain amount of processing and repackaging, the new products were marketed as the defendant's product.

The lower court had enjoined the activity, but the Supreme Court ruled that the outright injunction went too far, and observed that the plaintiff could neither prevent nor complain of the defendant's stating the nature of the component parts and their ultimate source, so long as the trademark was not used in the process. In so ruling, the high court raised the rhetorical question of what new rights trademark confers. According to the court, trademark does not confer a right to prohibit its use except to the extent requisite to protecting the owner's goodwill against the sale of the trademarked product as his.[11]

More than twenty years later the Supreme Court carried this rather surprising repackaging authorization one step further.[12] In this instance the defendant was collecting used Champion spark plugs for resale after repair and reconditioning. This time the defendant did retain the Champion name and other materials in its own packaging. Some of the material was essentially illegible, namely references to the defendant's reclamation effort. Both the trial and the appellate courts found trademark infringement and unfair competition. But the ultimate court order, affirmed by the Supreme Court, actually allowed the defendant to continue, subject only to a package labelling requirement, intended to avoid confusion between the new and reclaimed products. The defendant was allowed to retain the name Champion on his own labels.

The Supreme Court reasoned that even inferiority would be immaterial, so long as the defendant clearly and distinctively labelled his product as repaired or reconditioned. But, in fact, it had been found that Champion had not established any inferior qualities. Full disclosure on the packaging provided Champion with adequate protection. It is important to note in passing that there was also no showing of fraud or of palming off of the defendant's product as Champion's.

Two comparable cases of literary origin, insofar as commercials can be so characterized, have recently given rise to similar results in the federal courts in New York. In the Second Circuit, television commercials quoting from *Consumer Reports* were held to constitute neither copyright infringement nor trademark appropriation.[13]

The case was an appeal from a grant of preliminary injunction forbidding the defendants' use of the quotations from an article in the plaintiffs' publication in which the former's product was highly praised. The material at issue, identified as a quotation, was accompanied by a disclaimer of any affiliation with or endorsement by the plaintiffs.

The defendants asserted the fair use defense to the allegation of copyright infringement and asserted that the Lanham Act provided no basis for injunction. For a variety of reasons the court found the plaintiffs unlikely to prevail under copyright theory and proceeded to the trademark issues, analogous to those of the *Champion* precedent. The Second Circuit found no tendency to mislead or to confuse consumers. The disclaimer was found to counter either effect. The court declined to accede to the plaintiff's demand for a total ban on the use of its name. The lower court was reversed, and the preliminary injunction was vacated.

In the second case, the Southern District of New York addressed much the same controversy and provided some indication of how far the tolerance for another's incorporation of material subject to a trademark may go.[14] HBO was seeking a preliminary injunction against its competitor Showtime. The latter's commercials encouraged subscription to its cable services to complement that of HBO. HBO figured prominently in the commercials, and the plaintiff asserted that consumers would infer some merger or endorsement, despite express disclaimers similar to those utilized in the *Consumer Reports* situation. Plaintiff HBO based its trademark action on confusion and dilution.

The district court observed the direct competition between the parties: both serve the same marketplace with an identical type of service with programming that overlaps. In certain of the commercials, the court found insufficient likelihood of confusion to support a preliminary injunction. But in others, it found that the disclaimers were effectively nullified in context. In these commercials, there was doubt as to the identity of the actual sponsor. Of the three elements involved in dilution (a truly distinctive mark with secondary meaning among the public, debilitation of the trademark holder's selling power, and predatory intent) this district found the second to be absent. Thus, it declined to address the distinctiveness of HBO or the predatory intent of Showtime. Thus, preliminary injunction was entered only against those commercials which lent themselves to confusion.

The principles discussed here suggest that the name of a fictional character could be used in separate literary works without infringement so long as the sources were distinguished and effective disclaimers were present. Under such circumstances, there would be neither copyright nor trademark infringement. Cases addressing literary properties are, however, to the contrary, as will be discussed later in this chapter and in subsequent chapters addressing fictional characters themselves.

THE PUBLIC AS A PARTY IN TRADEMARK APPROPRIATION CASES

Trademark law is applied in an astonishing variety of situations. The application of basic trademark principles in these situations provides additional background for understanding their manifestation in the literary context as it is broadly defined here. The crucial underlying point cannot be overstated: "The consuming public is an unnamed third party in every action for trademark infringement."[15]

A suit for trademark infringement, then, advances two objectives: (1) protection of the proprietor's own pecuniary interest on the theory of unfair competition and (2) protection of the public against deception or lesser misrepresentations. While a trademark does not necessarily guarantee the consumer the highest quality, it does guarantee uniformity of quality at some recognized level. It is the means whereby the consumer can choose among competing products.[16] It should be obvious that these two objectives are not always going to be compatible, let alone consistent. It is consumer protection that takes precedence in the event of conflict.

The foundation of trademark law is based in consumer psychology. Legal decisions turn on what courts believe to be going on in the consumer's mind. Trademark infringement is recognized as a tort because it represents an interference in the marketing process. It is distinguishable from both patent and copyright infringement.

> The owner of a patent can exclude anyone else from making, using or selling the patented invention. A copyright proprietor can prevent anyone else from copying his work, either directly or in the form of a translation or adaptation. A trademark owner, on the other hand, has only the limited right to prohibit use of an identical or similar mark under circumstances where confusion, mistake or deception [is] likely to occur.[17]

Just how limited that right has become will be made abundantly clear in the course of reviewing the case law.

Though it is limited in scope, the exclusive property designated as trademark is subject to no time limits—so long as it is not abandoned by the proprietor.[18] Abandonment can either be actual or inferred from the factual situation. Significantly, it can actually be beyond the trademark proprietor's control.

> [T]rademarks must be handled with care, because improper use literally can destroy a trademark. If the consuming public comes to treat a trademark as the name for a type of product, rather than as a designation for one particular brand of product, the mark will no longer "identify" and "distinguish" the goods of one manufacturer. The trademark under these circumstances has become a generic term, which means it is available for anyone to use.[19]

The Coca Cola Company prevailed in an early case in which the presence of cocaine in the early formula presented an issue in equity.[20] Should a beverage containing a drug be protected? The Supreme Court observed:

> The name now characterizes a beverage to be had at almost any soda fountain. It means a single thing coming from a single source, and

well known to the community. . . . "Coca-Cola" probably means to most persons the plaintiff's familiar product to be had anywhere rather than a compound of particular substances.[21]

Many other trademarks have been subjected to intense judicial scrutiny. In a recent case, both the Nestle Company and the originator of the popular cookie claimed trademark rights to the Toll House name.[22] The court, upon review of the history of each claimant, allowed the defendant to continue to use the term so long as care was taken to inform the public as to source. In essence plaintiff Nestle had become a victim of its own phenomenal success and was itself guilty of using Toll House generically to indicate a type of cookie. Among the factors leading to this result was the dictionary entry in point. The contemporaneous *Webster's Dictionary* included both the original and the general use. This entry was treated as persuasive evidence of how a term is used and is understood by consumers.

In this modern technological era, a variety of products are being brought in to the trademark fold. Among them are items such as 3–D movie projection equipment;[23] electronic games, where the user of the game rather than its purchaser was considered for purposes of confusion;[24] posters, buttons, and patches relating to rock groups and performers;[25] and Ultracashmere trading on the goodwill of Ultrasuede.[26] In the last case, it was noted that action could be taken even though the source could be anonymous. Nevertheless, the court found confusion or dilution unlikely. (This court subsequently defined dilution as the "whittling away of an established trademark's distinctiveness, and hence its selling power, through its unauthorized placement on dissimilar products.")[27]

Even the space age has invaded the courts in a trademark infringement action.[28] The parties were toy manufacturers. *Battlestar Galactica* was once again involved, this time on the basis of competing uses of the word *galactic*. At issue was the ability to secure a trademark monopoly in words related to *galaxy*. The court took judicial notice of the popularity of the theme of spaceships, space warriors, and related subjects and of both *Star Wars* and *Star Trek* as well as of other such vehicles.[29] The court also noted that *galaxy* and its derivatives had been registered more than one hundred times since 1938.

At the time of the case, there were almost 50 applications pending and nearly ten nonregistered trademarks using *galaxy* or related terms in the toy field alone. Moreover, while *galactic* would be unusual and arbitrary in designating a dishwasher, vacuum cleaner, or the like, it was deemed a weak mark; i.e., more nearly generic than subject to secondary meaning, in the science fiction context represented by the competing lines of toys.

Before turning to the special application of trademark in literary and related works, especially where fictional characters are a component of legal analysis, a diversion is in order to examine an odd turn in recent case law.

THE ANTI-MONOPOLY CASES

First Appeal

This peculiar progression of cases represents a pitched legal battle between the familiar board game and a sort of counterculture newcomer. Challenge was issued by the proprietors of Anti-Monopoly, who directly attacked the validity of the Monopoly trademark. The odd turn commenced in 1979, when the Ninth Circuit remanded a district court's judgment for Monopoly for a determination of how the public actually uses that name.[30]

The lower court had, according to the Ninth Circuit, erroneously focused on whether the consuming public used the name in reference to a single game or to all real estate trading games. In effect, the Ninth Circuit was announcing for the first time that the proper question was instead whether public reference was to the game (product) or to its producer. And for purposes of preserving the trademark, reference to the latter was held a requisite.

If, in light of previous discussions, this finding of error comes as something of a surprise, the reader can well imagine the consternation that must have followed at General Mills. Since the patent had expired, the Monopoly proprietors had made substantial efforts to preserve the trademark, to keep it out of the public domain as a generic term. The court's reasoning was even more mystifying than the decision itself.

The Ninth Circuit started with this reading of generic: "[W]hen a trademark primarily denotes a product, not the product's producer, the trademark is lost.... [O]ne competitor will not be permitted to impoverish the language of commerce by preventing his fellows from fairly describing their own goods."[31] The court reiterated its novel requirement with the observation that even if only one producer (Parker Brothers) made the Monopoly game, and even though the public necessarily associates the product with that particular producer, the trademark is lost *unless source identification is its primary significance.*[32] In short, the Ninth Circuit is advancing the proposition that identification of source in a novel and highly specific sense is the only function trademark is designed to protect.

The Ninth Circuit, in apparent recognition of the new legal ground it was breaking, went to great lengths to explain itself. In doing so, it utilized the analogy of the relationship of *genus* to *species* to explain the relationship of *generic* to *specific*, but always with reference to the source rather than to the product. It used this example:

> Chessco's chess game is called EN PASSANT. When a consumer has available in his vocabulary the broad classifier "chess," but instead asks for EN PASSANT, we can infer that the consumer wants the "species" of chess equipment produced by Chessco. The consumer may have innumerable reasons for desiring EN PASSANT chess equipment: *e.g.* price, style, durability, consistency of quality, goodwill engendered by a catchy commercial jingle, or simply a liking for the sound of the trademark. But these desired characteristics are all source-particular, in that they correlate with a given producer, Chessco. The consumer uses the term EN PASSANT exactly as a trademark should be used—to enable him to recognize and ask for a particular producer's chess equipment. Moreover, Chessco benefits precisely as a producer should from a trademark: it reaps profits from consumer goodwill—both as to quality of its goods and attractiveness of its advertising—associated with its unique personality in the marketplace. It is important to recognize that the species term EN PASSANT subcategorizes only as to source. For trademark genericness purposes,

it is the source-denoting function of EN PASSANT which causes us to call EN PASSANT a species instead of a genus....

...[S]uppose Chessco's EN PASSANT has 81 instead of 64 squares. When a consumer calls for EN PASSANT, he may now be using the term EN PASSANT to describe game-relevant, but source-irrelevant, characteristics. That is, he wants EN PASSANT because it is a more interesting, longer game than regular chess, not because Chessco's board is more durable, stylized, cheaper, or consistent as to quality compared to other chess boards. To this consumer, EN PASSANT has become a unique game and he uses the word EN PASSANT primarily to describe a game played with 81 squares, not to describe who makes the game equipment. We thus cannot infer from the consumer's asking for EN PASSANT any preference as to the production source of the desired game. Where before there was only one relevant product category or genus, chess, there are now two: chess and EN PASSANT. If Chessco wants to monopolize this product category, it may do so through a patent, but not through a trademark. In trademark genericness parlance, EN PASSANT has evolved from a species to a genus.[33]

This convoluted reasoning loses much of its legitimacy if one accepts that there is one game known as Monopoly, with an array of specific features not found in comparable games. Monopoly is, in fact, not chess but En Passant. Producer and product are coextensive.

There are logical flaws in the court's reasoning. In the first instance, the hypothetical analogy of product genus and species is less than comparable. More important, this novel approach to protecting consumer interest appears likely to have quite the opposite effect.

Certainly most reasonable consumers who buy a brand name are looking for a product of known quality. They may or may not also be looking to the producer per se for that quality. In some cases they will not have the vaguest idea who the producer is. Why, if the public is to be protected, should consumers be held accountable for knowing who is behind the name of a product they want?

It is the rare consumer who will focus, as does the Ninth Circuit, on the source of the product rather than on its qualities, even when being selective. To most consumers, it is fortuitous that these qualities are source-particular. They deem them *brand*-particular. Consumers may well be sophisticated but not in the sense the court would protect. In fact brand loyalty suggests that product and producer somehow merge in a consumer's mind. If the brand name is representative of one or of the other, it had not previously mattered which was in the consumer's mind and probably should not. With stubborn perversity, the court seemed to be reasoning product recognition while actually requiring source identification.

Remand and Second Appeal

Having isolated the issue, the Ninth Circuit remanded to allow the trial court to address it. Many of the objections to the court's reasoning noted here obviously occurred to the proprietors of the name Monopoly—among others. In 1982 the case was again before the appellate court: once again the challenger had lost to Monopoly and once again the Ninth Circuit disagreed with the lower court.[34]

This time the appellate court found erroneous the finding that Monopoly denoted the game's producer to consumers. First, the efforts promoting and policing Monopoly were held insufficient protection in and of themselves. There is nothing novel in that position. But then the marketing surveys upon which General Mills was relying, according to the appellate court, failed to demonstrate that the word is *primarily* indicative of source. The court, unlike most laymen, was not convinced by evidence to the effect that even those who did not refer to their preference for Parker Brothers games, specifically Monopoly, did in fact want *the* game Monopoly. In fact, the court expressly rejected consumers' efforts to buy specific products such as Tide as appropriate recognition of trademark where consumers did not attribute Tide to Procter & Gamble in combination with a preference for Procter & Gamble products.

The U.S. Supreme Court

It should come as no surprise that the proprietors of Monopoly sought review of this result in the Supreme Court of the United States.[35] At issue was the Ninth Circuit's reasoning that source identification and product identification are mutually exclusive, with trademark survival dependent entirely on the former. Transcendent was the point that this novel doctrine ignores the realities of trademark in the marketplace. The corresponding contention was that the new test of loyalty to producer rather than product was placing the most successful trademarks in immediate jeopardy. The crucial point was that, unlike the earlier situations involving the products aspirin and cellophane, there is only one producer of Monopoly. Unfortunately for the orderly development of trademark principles, the Supreme Court refused to hear the appeal. More discussion followed in obvious puzzlement over the Supreme Court's refusal to grant certiorari.[36]

CONGRESSIONAL RESPONSE TO THE ANTI-MONOPOLY DECISIONS

The Anti-Monopoly cases did not lay the issues to rest. In early 1983 legislation was introduced in the U.S. Senate to repudiate the purchaser motivation test advanced by the Ninth Circuit.[37] The proposal was to find a trademark generic only when the consuming public clearly believes it fails to indicate the source. Presumably more would be required than simple failure to identify the source of a specific product being sought by names such as Tide, Coke, or Monopoly.[38] Later that same year a similar bill was introduced in the House. As finally passed, the Trademark Clarification Act of 1984, amending 15 U.S.C. 1064(c), reads:

> A registered mark shall not be deemed to be the common descriptive name of goods or services solely because such mark is also used as a name of or to identify a unique product or service. The primary significance of the registered mark to the relevant public rather than purchaser motivation shall be the test for determining whether the registered mark has become the common descriptive name of goods or services in connection with which it has been used.

Another, more recently popular board game, Trivial Pursuit, has found its way into court.[39] The U.S. maker of this highly successful game has filed suit to halt allegedly unauthorized sales of the Canadian "Baby Boomer" version in the United States. The plaintiff has the *exclusive* right to sell the game here. One suspects that avid pursuers of the game do not much care who it is coming from just as long as they can get it or some reasonable facsimile of it. It remains to be seen whether the action of Congress has actually undone the unique approach of the Ninth Circuit.

APPLICATION OF TRADEMARK PRINCIPLES TO LITERARY PROPERTIES

Some questions of considerable interest to artists and authors have arisen in trademark law. For example, can the name and portrait of a musical group comprise a trademark on sound recordings and corresponding album covers?[40] The court ruled that the name could but that the portrait could not (at least on the facts presented). The group AᗺBA argued that name and portrait indicated the source of the recordings and were a guaranty of quality as controlled by AᗺBA. It was further argued that the situation was analogous to the already acceptable trademark registration of a series title. The court, then, found AᗺBA itself akin to a series title, while the full name of each album, comparable to a single entry in a literary series, was not recognized as a trademark.

Trademark in Titles; the Requirement for Secondary Meaning

In fact unauthorized use of a title can be a violation of the Lanham Act.[41] But titles are protected only when they have acquired "secondary meaning," that is, where the public identifies the title with the proprietor and the underlying work. The U.S. Court of Customs and Patent Appeals has denied registration to a title of a single work.[42] The court of appeals agreed with the assistant commissioner of patents that a title is descriptive and that the author can have no property in it but did add that a trademark usage of the title would be distinguishable.

Each book and its title, then, are new and unique. The title merely describes the book. By way of contrast, a series title has acquired the requisite secondary meaning in that each book in the series comes from the same source because

> the name of the series is not descriptive of any one book and each book has its individual name or title. A series name is comparable to the title of a periodical publication such as a magazine or newspaper. While it may be indicative, either specifically or by association in the public mind, of the general nature of the contents of the publication, it is not the name or title of anything contained in it. A book title, on the other hand, especially one which is coined or arbitrary, identifies a specific literary work . . . and is not associated in the public mind with the publisher, printer or book-seller.[43]

In other words, the work is not associated with its manufacturer. Instead, it is probably associated with the author, who actually produced the literary work that the consumer intends to purchase. Furthermore, according to the court, the underlying individual copyrights will eventually enter the public domain. At that juncture, use of the corresponding titles cannot be withheld on the theory of trademark.

Note that the title of a magazine, a series of publications associated with a specific source, is protected. In one case in New York, the district court entered a preliminary injunction precluding publication of a magazine, *Fantastica*, which was likely to be confused with the plaintiff's *Fantastic Films*, even though the target audiences were not identical and the defendant's magazine would also bear the legend, "Starlog presents."[44]

In some situations, however, titles of individual works have acquired the secondary meaning required for protection. The novel *$E=MC^2$, Mon Amour* was adapted as a film under the title *A Little Romance*. The defendant, Dell Publishing, negotiated for the English translation and paperback rights, including the right to market the book under any title. Because the film departed substantially from the original novel, the plaintiff, Orion Pictures, declined to enter Dell's marketing strategy. Dell on its part declined to publish a novel based on the screenplay.

When Dell eventually published its translation, the cinema title was used along with the familiar notice "now a major motion picture." In seeking a preliminary injunction, Orion Pictures claimed that the publication would diminish the popularity of the film.[45] At issue was whether the title, *A Little Romance*, had acquired secondary meaning. In order to resolve the issue, the court asked whether the ordinary prudent purchaser would be confused or actively misled as to the source of the goods. In an astute declaration, the New York district answered its own question in the affirmative.

Clearly, it observed, no consumer could literally confuse the book with the movie. But consumers are interested in the relationships across media. While anyone buying the book after seeing the movie would, upon careful study of the credits, be able to distinguish the original work from the novelization, the likely assumption would be that the original book bore a very close resemblance to the film, especially in light of the promotion. On the other hand, someone attending the movie after reading the book would be surprised at the differences between the two. Because the defendant's book, by virtue of its title and inscription, gave the impression that it was the novelization of the film and, therefore, similar to it, the defendant's promotion had misled the public.[46] The defendant's book was derivative of the original novel but not of the film. Future use of the title was enjoined as was use of other materials suggesting more of a relationship between the book and the film than existed in fact.

A similar situation arose surrounding the Disney film, *The Black Hole*.[47] When the film was entitled *The Black Hole in Space*, during prerelease publicity, Disney licensed that title for merchandise, including the game giving rise to the suit. Each party sued the other on theories of unfair competition, trademark infringement and false designation of origin. In the end priority of use became the deciding issue. The arguments were equitable in nature, and the likelihood of confusion was acknowledged by both parties. The court rather neatly allowed the game to be entitled Hole in Space.

Jaws similarly has been recognized as a legitimate trademark for entertainment services and merchandise.[48] Thus,

Montgomery Ward's artful use of the word in association with food disposers was held to be misappropriation subject to an order to cease such usage. The issue was dilution, demonstrated in no small part by the defendant's choice of the term for the particular merchandise in question. Here the court expanded on the confusion concept to include the likelihood of a public inference of approval, association, or sponsorship. Confusion did not require evidence to the effect that the offending merchandise was believed to be an actual product of Universal Studios.

Case law focuses primarily on conceptions of character where trademark issues arise from the content of literary properties. Some of the judicial reluctance to enter a fray deemed novel is illustrated in a case involving television commercials.[49] At issue was the "Be a Pepper" campaign of the plaintiff, Dr. Pepper.

The defendant, Sambo's Restaurant, had developed a "Dancing Seniors" campaign—an attempted parody of the original—with the advice of counsel, in tacit acknowledgment of the risks involved. The court found no trademark violation, but copyright infringement (leading to a shortening of the Dr. Pepper campaign and a loss of goodwill) did exist despite the defendant's fair use contention. Given the abbreviated format of commercials, this case necessarily turns on content with the emphasis at least implicitly on the characters presented in the two works.

A case more obviously addressing character was brought by the cheerleading squad of the Dallas Cowboys against the film, *Debbie Does Dallas*.[50] The Dallas Cheerleaders fostered a particular public image that depended at least in part on high standards of moral character. The film, as might be expected in a movie in which the principal is dubbed Pussycat, was one of sexploitation. The plaintiff claimed misappropriation with confusion and dilution of quality while the defendant advanced the parody defense and the remote likelihood that anyone would believe the plaintiff could be the source of the film. The defendant's defenses failed. The decision turned on use of the Dallas uniform as a trademark, here a significant aspect of the characters presented to the public by the respective parties. The court had some interesting observations regarding that crucial third party to the action:

> In considering the question of whether there is a tendency to deceive or a likelihood of confusion within the purview of the statute, it must be realized that the buying public includes the unthinking and credulous. The public cannot be expected to analyze or carefully weigh what is presented to them in promotion and advertisements. The question is what is the likely ultimate *impression*, upon customers of the relevant services and products which will be created by what is said and what is reasonably implied.[51]

King Kong is a character both obviously and frequently subject to trademark litigation. While the deLaurentiis version of the horror classic was being made, a film entitled *Ape* was being publicized.[52] The case arose when an agent for *King Kong* ordered promotional posters and instead received posters for *Ape*. The plaintiff felt the poster to show an imitation of King Kong, despite carefully drawn differences. In requiring modifications of the *Ape* posters, the court reiterated four factors to be addressed in deciding and ordering relief in an infringement action: (1) secondary meaning, (2) likelihood of confusion, (3) the probability of an attempt to palm off, and (4) diversion of business. The order requiring modification went no further in penalizing the defendant because the last factor was of minimal impact in this particular case.

King Kong came back to court to face Donkey Kong.[53] This time the legal issues were substantially more convoluted. According to the court, the key to the morass of rights was to be found in the identity and image of King Kong. The defenses raised are highly significant to trademark in character, primarily: Can King Kong denote a single source of origin in that it (he?) originated as a book and magazine serial; has been subjected to some fifteen licenses of the name, character, and story; is the subject of additional usages and third-party trademark registrations; and is defined in various dictionaries and listed in some editions of *Roget's Thesaurus*? There were additional complications regarding the source or sources of King

Kong, but the foregoing are the most important to understanding the application of trademark law to characters.

After an exhaustive review of just who King Kong is, the court turned its attention to Donkey Kong. When development of the game began in 1981, the character was not a gorilla. That specific creature evolved through more than one design change. Only after the creature was established, was the name attached. *Kong* denotes *a* gorilla. *Donkey* is a translation for a Japanese term suggesting stupidity of the goofy variety.

The court held that King Kong lacks secondary meaning as a matter of law. There was no dispute to be addressed. Here was a situation in which the character had become too popular. The proprietor thereby lost control, because of competing property interests in King Kong. Further, because of unauthorized uses of King Kong trademarks for various purposes, King Kong no longer signifies a single source of origin to consumers. Thus, it is no longer a valid trademark.

Although the public need not know the name of the manufacturer that produces the trademarked product for purposes of secondary meaning, the public must be aware that the product does derive from a *single* source.[54] In the event of reversal on appeal, the court also expressly held further that, even if Universal Studios possessed a valid trademark, there was no likelihood of confusion between King Kong and Donkey Kong.

COMPLEMENTARY PROTECTION OF FICTIONAL CHARACTERS

In the remaining chapters, legally recognized properties in characters will be considered in greater depth. The extent to which they are protected by copyright and trademark law and through related concepts of unfair competition will be examined. The implications of relevant limitations will be considered in the context of the complementary aspects of the pertinent legal principles. Then, these analyses will be synthesized into a proposal for reconciliation of precedent, particularly in the crucial Second and Ninth Circuits, which respectively afford and deny copyright in characters. More important, the synthesis will provide a framework for predicting whether a given character is likely to enjoy copyright protection.

NOTES

1. The Lanham Act: 15 U.S.C. 1051–1072, 1091–1096, 1111–1121, 1123–1127. *See* 15 U.S.C. 1125, 1127.
2. Bayer Co. v. United Drug Co., 272 F. 505 (S.D. N.Y. 1921).
3. 272 F. at 509.
4. DuPont Cellophane Co. v. Waxed Products Co., 85 F.2d 75 (2d Cir. 1936).
5. 85 F.2d at 77.
6. 85 F.2d at 81.
7. Feathercombs v. Solo Products Corporation, 306 F.2d 251 (2d Cir. 1962).
8. 306 F.2d at 256.
9. 306 F.2d at 257.
10. Prestonettes v. Coty, 44 S. Ct. 350, 264 U.S. 359 (1924).
11. 44 S. Ct. at 351.
12. Champion Spark Plug v. Sanders, 67 S. Ct. 1136, 331 U.S. 125 (1947).
13. Consumers Union of U.S. v. General Signal Corp., 724 F.2d 1044 (2d Cir. 1983).
14. Home Box Office v. Showtime/The Movie Channel, 665 F. Supp. 1079 (S.D. N.Y. 1987).
15. Diamond, *The Public Interest and the Trademark System*, 62 J. PAT. OFF. SOC'Y 528 (1980), at 529.
16. Ibid.
17. Ibid., at 532.
18. Diamond, *Properly Used, Trademarks Are Forever*, 68 A.B.A. J. 1575 (1982).
19. Ibid., at 1576.
20. Coca Cola v. Koke Co., 254 U.S. 143, 41 S. Ct. 113 (1920).
21. 41 S. Ct. at 114.
22. The Nestle Company v. Chester's Market, 219 U.S.P.Q. 298 (D. Conn. 1983).
23. Filmways Pictures v. Marks Polarized Corp., 320 U.S.P.Q. 870 (S.D. N.Y. 1982).
24. Midway Mfg. Co. v. Bandai-America, 216 U.S.P.Q. 812 (S.D. N.Y. 1982).
25. Bi-Rite Enterprises v. Button Master, 217 U.S.P.Q. 910 (S.D. N.Y. 1983).

26. Spring Mills v. Ultracashmere House, 215 U.S.P.Q. 1057 (S.D. N.Y. 1982).

27. 217 U.S.P.Q. at 916.

28. Mego Corp. v. Mattel, 203 U.S.P.Q. 377 (S.D. N.Y. 1978).

29. 203 U.S.P.Q. at 379.

30. Anti-Monopoly, Inc. v. General Mills Fun Group, 611 F.2d 296 (9th Cir. 1979).

31. 611 F.2d at 301.

32. 611 F.2d at 302.

33. 611 F.2d at 303.

34. Anti-Monopoly, Inc. v. General Mills Fun Group, 684 F.2d 1316 (9th Cir. 1982).

35. 25 PAT. TRADEMARK & COPYRIGHT J. (BNA) 189 (January 6, 1983).

36. *See, e.g.*, 25 PAT. TRADEMARK & COPYRIGHT J. (BNA) 351 (February 24, 1983), 507 (April 21, 1983).

37. 25 PAT. TRADEMARK & COPYRIGHT J. (BNA) 165 (June 16, 1983).

38. Bill Would Clarify Genericness Test and Extend CAFC's Jurisdiction, 27 PAT. TRADEMARK & COPYRIGHT J. 135 (December 8, 1983).

39. *See* Selchow & Righter Co. v. Decipher, 598 F. Supp. 1489 (E.D. Va. 1984); Selchow & Righter Co. v. Goldex Corp., 612 F. Supp. 19 (S.D. Fla. 1985).

40. In re Polar Music International, 221 U.S.P.Q. 315 (Fed. Cir. 1983).

41. Davis v. United Artists, 547 F. Supp. 722 (S.D. N.Y. 1982).

42. Application of Cooper, 254 F.2d 611 (C.C.P.A. 1958).

43. 254 F.2d at 615–616.

44. *See* Blake Publishing Corp. v. O'Quinn Studios, 202 U.S.P.Q. 848 (S.D. N.Y. 1979).

45. Orion Pictures Co. v. Dell Pub. Co., 471 F. Supp. 392 (S.D. N.Y. 1979).

46. 471 F. Supp. at 397.

47. Walt Disney Productions v. Kusan, 204 U.S.P.Q. 284 (C.D. Cal. 1979).

48. Universal City Studios v. Montgomery Ward & Co., 207 U.S.P.Q. 852 (N.D. Ill. 1980).

49. Dr. Pepper Co. v. Sambo's Restaurants, 517 F. Supp. 1202 (N.D. Tex. 1981).

50. Dallas Cowboys Cheerleaders v. Pussycat Cinema, 467 F. Supp. 366 (S.D. N.Y. 1979).

51. 467 F. Supp. at 374.

52. Paramount Pictures v. Worldwide Entertainment Corp., 195 U.S.P.Q. 539 (S.D. N.Y. 1977).
53. Universal City Studios v. Nintendo Co., 578 F. Supp. 911 (S.D. N.Y. 1983).
54. 578 F. Supp. at 923.

Part II

Character as an Intellectual Property

5

Character as a Copyright or Trademark Property

ELEMENTS OF COPYRIGHT AND TRADEMARK

In proceeding from the principles behind protection of intellectual properties by copyright and trademark into application to fictional characters, it is essential to recall the basics of the two types of property. The elements of copyright start with copyrightability of and copyright in the work. It must be shown that, despite associated traditions behind this work, its expression is unique and that the allegedly infringing work has taken that expression. Thus, the source of the allegedly infringing work must be the earlier work and not the underlying tradition or some independent source. Since actual direct copying is rare, infringement must be inferred from access to the earlier work and substantial similarity in the expression of the two works. Ideas are judicially compared through the objective extrinsic test while expression is compared through the more subjective intrinsic test.

Characters are subject to no different approach; therefore, substantial similarity between characters may occur without infringement if they are a part of scènes à faire. Substantial similarity may also be defensible when it constitutes fair use, particularly in the form of parody. But the question remains whether characters are in fact copyrightable and subject to independent infringement where there is substantial similarity beyond scènes à faire and exceeding fair use. The case law remains seemingly unsettled despite more than thirty years of law and commentary.[1]

Trademark in this context is complementary to copyright in that trademark protects names and images on behalf of the proprietor and in the interests of the consuming public. Trademark is invoked where there is identity or confusing similarity between two marks. Characters, as well as certain titles, are subject to trademark protection and to sanctions where unfair competition can be established. Because a trademark is indicative of the source of the marked product, intended or innocent confusion in the public mind is the foundation of an actionable wrong. Moreover, dilution of the effectiveness of a trademark in indicating a sole source is actionable.

Arguably, trademark protection can preserve a character indefinitely, even beyond the lifetime of an associated copyright, but the trademark can be abandoned by its proprietor in actuality or through public treatment of the mark, notwithstanding a concerted effort on the part of the proprietor to retain control. Popular fictional characters are particularly vulnerable to usurpation, not only through misappropriation by other artists but also by the hand of the consuming public—the very fandom through which popularity has been established.

This and subsequent chapters will review cases in which misappropriation is alleged. Chapters 6 and 7 will also consider in greater detail the effect of public usurpation of control over the destiny of heroes in the popular arts.

COPYRIGHT IN FICTIONAL CHARACTERS

For all the expected interest in preserving rights in fictional characters, the Copyright Act is silent on the matter. The act neither includes characters in the subject matter[2] of copyright nor lists them either among the exclusive rights[3] or among violations of those rights.[4] In fact, *character* is not to be found in the index to Title 17 or in the indices to the Notes of Decisions for the referenced sections. Nimmer and Nimmer briefly address characters in a single section of their treatise. The discussion spans no more than a few pages of the four volumes.[5]

Theory and Early Cases

Theory and comment. In order to understand the extent to which characters can be protected by copyright, it is necessary to recall that an idea is not protected but that its expression is protected. Thus, it is essential to determine where characters stand on the theoretical continuum by which expression is ultimately connected to idea. The practical significance of such determinations becomes clear when a fictional character is removed from its original setting and carried forward in new vehicles. John Rambo, for example, was initially established in David Morrell's novel, *First Blood.* At the climax Rambo is put to death—as a mercy—by his fictional creator, Colonel Trautman, who had trained him in guerrilla tactics. In the film version Rambo survives. But before he could proceed into the film sequels, a legal accommodation distributing rights to the character had to be reached with Morrell.[6] In Morrell's novelization of the first sequel, there is a brief note to the effect that, while Rambo had died in the novel, he survived in the film.[7]

Yankwich points to the determination of an English jurist to the effect that more than characterization alone (the broad description of the character per se) must be taken.[8] To justify the charge that a new character is not original but an infringement, the incidents and situations through which that character expresses itself must also have been taken.

In theory, at least, where character infringement is at issue, the omission of any one of three elements of character (viz., characterization, actions, reactions) reduces the property taken to either an idea or a component of scènes à faire falling between idea and its expression.[9] As the cases reveal, neither is protected under copyright law. Thus, the aggrieved proprietor of a persona, for which the status of an independent literary property is sought, bears a heavy burden in seeking to establish the taking of all the pieces comprising the character. Furthermore, this independent literary property, once established, must itself be both original and uniquely distinguishable from all pretenders.

In practice it would seem nearly impossible to establish the taking of a character absent the taking of an entire series of comics, of all the elements of a film, or of an entire novel. Given that neither characterization nor reactions alone can be sufficient to establish a character; what amount of taking of the components is sufficient to establish the three necessary elements, where the work itself is not subject to an infringement action? Put more succinctly: Can a character be independently subject to copyright at all?[10]

Behind the requisite demonstration of a taking of all the necessary components of character is the additional requirement that the incidents and situations that blend into the unique character themselves be original (or at least represent an original combination). Where those incidents and situations were already old and well established prior to publication of the proprietor's property, there can be no invasion of a legal right, because such materials are already in the public domain.

The aggrieved party indeed faces a herculean task. There are people, after all, who assert with some justification that there is nothing new under the sun (or, for that matter, *beyond* our sun—in the case of works of science fiction or fantasy). Anyone who seeks to locate that elusive point of demarcation separating character from mere characterization and thus separating the zone of protection from the public domain is faced with a task no less daunting.

Early case law. Protection of characters, such as it may be, is of relatively recent advent, and its placement in the historical context of case law is most revealing. Many of the cases reflect the added complication of alleged infringement across media—usually from the printed word to the performing arts (written image to visual presentation).

The basic issue, once again, is whether the "new" character is taken from the previous literary incarnation or has emerged from the later author's imagination. Both characters may well have evolved (in parallel) from the same roots. If they did not emerge independently, resolution depends on whether the "old" character is protected or in the public domain. The old and new characters usually share the same name. Thus, as will be developed in chapters 6 and 7, trademark law complements copyright in protecting a popular character.

The cases indicate that the argument claiming a persona (characterization) in fact to have been transported into character and, thus, expression is most easily supported in the case of the comics and those familiar vignettes: television commercials.

The 1909 Copyright Act quite understandably made no express reference to the cinema. Photoplays and other motion pictures were not expressly protected until 1912, when, oddly, soundtracks still went unmentioned. (When sound recordings were added in 1971, there was an assumption that soundtracks were an integral part of motion pictures.) With the 1976 amendments any tangible medium of expression became subject to statutory protection, with a nonexhaustive list of examples.[11]

Throughout early case law development, the focus was on storytelling to the exclusion of other modes of expression, and the reasoning behind the decisions relied heavily on a rather inadequate judicial literary analysis. As critics, it might be argued, the triers of fact and law made good jurists. Thus, the *Krofft* case, discussed in Chapter 2, represents an important landmark along the road to character protection. This decision recognized that a protected work of television and cinema does more than tell a story.

> Its simultaneous presentation of two-dimensional sights and sounds engages most of the senses of its audience in a unique manner. A film's aural and visual modes of expression interact to form a synthesis that transcends those modes. The look, sound, and "feel" of a movie often have a greater impact on the audience than its story.[12]

One need only recall the respective impacts of *Frankenstein*, *The Exorcist*, and *Star Wars* to recognize the truth of the foregoing observation.[13] It is reasonable then to expect the courts to go beyond literary aspects of such works in their analyses in order to afford adequate legal protection to audiovisual products having great commercial value (and, significantly, both a limited time to impress the audience—usually two hours or less—and a relatively short life expectancy—often a matter of days, hours, or even minutes—on the screen). Among the courts' additional considerations are the soundtrack and characters.

Legal analysis of characters had been similarly limited. Initially at least, characters as such were generally held to be uncopyrightable. The only circumstances in which a character was protected were those in which the character was in essence the equivalent of (coextensive with) the story.[14] More recently, however, protection has been extended to cartoon characters, at least in audiovisual works, but not without a paradox:

> On the one hand, the more "human" the character, . . . the less likely that he or she will be found to be . . . sufficiently delineated to merit separate copyright protection. On the other hand, if presented in a science fiction, space, or horror setting, with the attendant visual and aural trappings, even the most simplistic and simple-minded of characters, with all due respect to "R2–D2" and "Pufnstuf," have a strong claim for copyright protection.[15]

Examples of cases involving characters go all the way back to 1914 and the cartoon characters Mutt and Jeff. This early decision reflected alleged infringement across media, in this case from printed cartoons to a dramatic performance.[16] The cartoons were copyrighted, and the complainant was the exclusive licensee of the associated dramatic rights. The defendant's *In Cartoonland* included one "Nutt" and one "Giff" who were quite obviously intended and understood to be Mutt and Jeff. In addition to being costumed and madeup to suggest the cartoon characters, the live surrogates quoted striking catchwords and other dialogue that was in harmony with the original work.

Against a defense of parody or burlesque, the district court held that Nutt and Giff did injure the copyrighted material. Significantly, the New York court noted that once people had seen the copy, they would not be more likely to spend money to see the licensed work (should it ever materialize), because "a good many of them would probably think they had already seen those characters."[17] It is reasonably obvious here that Mutt and Jeff are, for all intents and purposes, the work or the expression; that is, coextensive with the work as a whole.

In another early case the author of *Stella Dallas* sued NBC for misappropriation of title, personality, and established goodwill.[18] The author, who was contemplating a sequel, sought to halt the production of the defendant's radio skits based on episodes in the life of the heroine as both inferior and not based directly or indirectly on the novel. The skits were "of such inferior grade as to imperil the further sale of said novel and of any sequel . . . and the reputation of the complainant . . . and thereby to imperil the further sale of other works."[19]

That the plaintiff had stated a cause of action under copyright principles is reflected in the court's denial of the motion to dismiss. But only evidence established in the course of a trial would have revealed where Stella Dallas stood in the continuum carrying character from idea to expression. Surely, however, she is beyond a mere cartoon, more than simplistic and simple minded in execution.

Sam Spade and the Ninth Circuit

The case most often referenced in the context of copyright protection of characters revolved around Dashiell Hammett's Sam Spade.[20] The case has more than one interesting twist: The author, Hammett, had assigned the entire copyright in *The Maltese Falcon* to Warner Bros. Hammett continued to use the Sam Spade character and had contracted with others for use of the character. There was, for example, the radio show, *Adventures of Sam Spade*. As proprietor of all rights under the copyright of *The Maltese Falcon*, Warner Bros. sued Hammett for infringement. Hammett denied the claim and sued for a declaration of his rights to the character.

The trial court held that Hammett, even in assigning the entire copyright, retained the right to the Sam Spade character. In deciding Hammett had retained the right to continue his own use of the character, the court alluded to Warner Bros.' ability to negotiate a contract to serve its needs on the one hand and the readers' continuing interest in the character on the other. The original proprietor of the character was not trying to prevent infringement by another. Instead, the proprietor was fighting to retain his own right to the character and the character's name. In doing so Hammett pointed to the custom and practice of the mystery-writer's trade.

The appellate court expanded the trial court's reasoning to include the intent of the copyright statute in reasoning that

> [i]f Congress had intended that the sale of the right to publish a copyrighted story would foreclose the author's use of its characters in subsequent works for the life of the copyright, it would seem Congress would have made specific provisions therefor. [In fact the statute did not specifically mention characters or their names.] The characters of an author's imagination and the art of his descriptive talent, like a painter's or like a person with his penmanship, are always limited and always fall into limited patterns. . . .
>
> We conclude that even if the Owners assigned their complete rights in the copyright . . . such assignment did not prevent the author from using the characters used therein, in other stories. The characters were vehicles for the story told, and the vehicles did not go with the sale of the story.[21]

In regard to the unfair competition issue, also raised, the appellate court further reasoned:

> It is patent that the characters of The Maltese Falcon could not fairly be used in such a manner as to cause the Falcon to be materially lessened in its commercial worth by degrading or cheapening them so that the public would not be interested in their capers. They could not be used in such a manner as to deceive the public or to "palm off" to the public the idea that they were really witnessing The Maltese Falcon when they viewed showings of the other stories.[22]

This case is frequently cited to support the proposition that character is uncopyrightable. Even though this case may support such a proposition, the proposition is wrong: "If someone other than Hammett had used Sam Spade, or a character like Sam Spade with a different name, Warner Brothers [*sic.*] would have won. And the court would have said that the use of Sam Spade was a violation of copyright."[23]

In fact, it would appear that both litigants were served: Warner Bros. has exclusive rights to *The Maltese Falcon*; rights protected even against the original author. On the other hand, the creator of Sam Spade has retained his right to continue Spade's adventures in a variety of media, so long as he does not infringe on that one particular work. Equity is served. And it would appear that a character is a protected property, independent of the copyright in the work itself.

Copyright, like all properties, consists of a bundle of rights. If Sam Spade was not included in the bundle for all purposes but remains in the hands of the author for future use, the character must be a separable property. Logically, if Sam Spade is not subject to a separate copyright, he is some novel form of property. The question is how that separate property is to be identified.

The significance of the question of how characters are to be protected, especially in the jurisprudence of California, is reflected in the problems associated with the 1989 Academy Award ceremony.[24] The Disney character Snow White made what can only be described as an ill-advised appearance in the opening production number. Not only was the appearance lambasted by critics, it gave rise to some strong communications out of the Disney organization. When the demanded apology was not forthcoming, Disney filed suit based in copyright infringement, unfair competition, and dilution of business reputation (a trademark claim). The academy had neglected to secure the right to use the character. There was nothing comical or trivial about the situation despite the humor most, more distanced, observers appreciated.

AFTER SAM SPADE: COPYRIGHT IN CHARACTERS?

Francis, the talking mule, gave rise to a tax case turning in part on whether the character was independently subject to copyright.[25] The intricacies of the federal taxation laws of the fifties are not of concern here, but the matter of copyright was significant to the tax to be paid on the sale of certain intellectual properties, including Francis, to Universal. The Eastern District of Louisiana held Francis to be inseparable from the literary works in that the character took both definition and delineation from the book. In short, the literary description in the book composes the entire character, and without this description of his mannerisms, his manifestations, Francis would cease to exist. To the extent that Francis has sufficient form and substance to be considered property, that existence is exclusively attributable to the literary composition.[26]

For tax purposes at least, Francis is subject to copyright but equivalent to the story. From the court's reasoning as noted, it is difficult to imagine when a character would not be coextensive with the copyrighted work, but, admittedly, Francis is unique and something of a cartoon figure. Certainly, he is not human with all the associated complexities of the most shallowly drawn human character.

In the Courts of the Ninth Circuit

Regan. In recent years, a character, at least arguably more human than Francis, was expressly found not to be protected by copyright. She is the child, Regan, of the film *The Exorcist.*[27] A preliminary injunction was sought for alleged infringement perpetrated by the film *Beyond the Door.* At issue was not only the character Regan but also the array of special effects primarily involving Regan. The district court started with the proposition that characters in a (screen)play are not ordinarily protectible.

From that proposition the court held that Regan herself did not come within the protectible exception of a distinctively delineated character whose delineation was copied. The reasoning was that the film was itself subordinate to the character. And even if subordination had not been found, according to the court, there were significant distinctions between the two characters at issue. Regan was a demure child turned into a profane monster and saved by religious exorcism. The allegedly infringing character was a mature woman beset by abnormal fetal development unassociated with any religious connotations.[28] Finally, the court observed that the special effects in the defendants' film were typical theatrical tricks long in use. Hence, only the ads for *Beyond the Door* were found to be an infringement. The court seemed to suggest that the character Regan rises above the work but not so far as to be independent of it. The ruling indicates some inclination among courts of the

Ninth Circuit to bring characters frankly within the ambit of copyright.

The A-Team. Comparable results arose in the Ninth Circuit itself when a copyright action was brought against the creators of the television series *The A-Team.*[29] The jury had found substantial similarities between the series and the plaintiff's script for the television pilot *Cargo.* The trial court, however, had entered a judgment notwithstanding the verdict, which the Ninth Circuit affirmed. Both works centered around Vietnam veterans who engaged in comedic action-adventures starting from a premise of apparently felonious past activities. In general, the similar concepts and components of the two works were held to be no more than scènes à faire.

The case for infringement was found to be strongest, however, with regard to the respective characters.[30] Here the appellate court allowed for the possibility of finding some parallels between five pairs of characters. But the court hastened to add that the action could not be maintained, with express reference to the Sam Spade decision. It did acknowledge other cases allowing for copyright infringement where characters were particularly distinctive, in the Ninth Circuit (specifically Disney cartoon characters) as well as the Second Circuit (Superman among others).[31] But the A-Team characters failed to rise to the level of delineation required even by the more lenient standard applied in the Second Circuit. The plaintiff's characters were limited to summaries of only a few lines with an identification of the actor intended to play them. In short, character delineation in this case was insufficient, both individually and in ensemble, to give rise to any reconsideration of the Sam Spade opinion.[32] Once again there is the hint of some willingness for the Ninth Circuit to retrench on this important issue.

In the Courts of the Second Circuit

Cast and crew of WKRP. In 1982, between the two foregoing decisions, an episode of the television series *WKRP in Cincinnati* was under consideration in the Second Circuit.[33] The plaintiff, whose radio script was allegedly infringed by the episode, was seeking summary judgment on the contention of substantial similarity as a matter of law. But it was the defendant's cross motion for dismissal that was granted.

Acknowledging that the dichotomy between idea and expression is vague and that no general principle exists to determine when an imitation has gone beyond the idea into expression, the court proceeded to address both action and characterization. It was held that, even if the premise of the episode in question had been copied, it alone is an idea. There was no substantial similarity in its expression; that is, in its handling and in the scenes, details, and characterization in the two works. The plaintiffs' characters were dismissed as types with little development:

> [P]laintiffs' characters are too undeveloped to permit protection, and even those characters in defendant's show, who exhibit a surface similarity to plaintiffs' because they share the same role (station owner, engineer or newscaster), have been clearly shown to be too dissimilar in treatment to permit an inference that defendant took their "expression" from plaintiffs.[34]

Hopalong Cassidy. At the same time, Hopalong Cassidy was also before the New York courts.[35] The plaintiff, Filmvideo, sought a declaratory judgment finding both the Hopalong Cassidy books and twenty-three films to be in the public domain, allowing Filmvideo to license the films to television. The respondent, successor to the author of the books, counterclaimed for an injunction and damages, with an allegation of copyright infringement, in that the films were based on the books. The book copyrights had been properly renewed pursuant to the legislative amendments, but the film copyrights had not. The question before the Southern District of New York was whether the films constituted infringements of the books. Put another way, was the taking substantial or no more than fair use?

The character, Hopalong Cassidy, had been established in seventeen books written between 1907 and 1935. Since then the books' copyright renewals had been obtained and were in effect. On the other hand, copyrights in the seventeen "Hoppy" films, of which Paramount was proprietor by an agreement with the author of the books, had expired.

Following these expirations, a third party purchased the negatives, subject to contractual restrictions on their exhibition. In court the purchaser sought a judgment declaring the renewal of the copyrights in the underlying books to be invalid. The contention was that either the books or the films were in the public domain; therefore the films were free of the contract restrictions and could be shown on television. The defendants filed a counterclaim to enjoin the use of the properties on television.

In the first case brought by Filmvideo, the issue was whether the copyrights in the books could be infringed by a showing of the films which were in the public domain. In the first instance, there was no doubt that a film could infringe a novel. Further, it was held, failure to renew copyrights in the films was not in effect an abandonment of copyrights in the corresponding books.

In the second case, the purchaser proceeded to argue that the films represented new material and, thus, were not derivative of the existing works subject to claims of infringement. The proprietors of the existing copyrights countered that each film was based on one of the books. The court held that, in order to be successful, the proprietors must not only demonstrate the requisite similarity but also address relevant contractual provisions.

Recognizing certain unavoidable differences between a film and the book being adapted based on obvious differences in the media of expression, the New York district observed that film breathes life into certain characters through speeches and actions conveying the same or similar messages as the underlying text. Here characterization was a part of the license at issue and, thus, infringement was found in character names and development among numerous other items. In short, as was the case with Sam Spade, the original characters are retained by the original author, and that author is protected—but this time expressly by copyright principles. (But, note that the character here again is implicitly inseparable from the works.)[36]

Amos and Andy. Building from the reasoning in the preceding case, this same New York district identified as a novel question the specific issue of whether "characters that are in the public domain in a literary work [are] protectable by copyright in an audiovisual presentation."[37] The plaintiff, having failed in the effort to secure literary rights to use components of old *Amos & Andy* radio scripts in a Broadway musical comedy, went forward with the vehicle with the apparent intent of establishing those rights in court. His action for declaratory judgment was filed; countersuit by CBS on copyright and trademark followed. The matter was before the court on CBS's motion for summary judgment dismissing the action and determining liability.

The radio show, opening in 1928, had been transferred to CBS twenty years later. The show remained on the air until 1955. CBS ran it on television from 1951 through 1953, and it remained in syndication until 1966. The scripts from 1928 through 1948 were in the public domain.

In response to the novel question regarding characters, the court held that they were protected by both copyright and trademark. As to copyright, the court held that the audiovisual works constituted visual representations of the characters on film. Those representations were in effect expression going beyond word portraits. Although that fact was not abrogated in the transfer across media, the court declined to decide the matter of infringement in advance. The material factual question of infringement would depend upon the stage presentations themselves; therefore, liability could not yet be established. Note that this same court found characters in the film based on a murder previously fictionalized in the novel, *Looking for Mr. Goodbar*, not to have been taken from the novel. In this instance the characters at issue were all individuals who had been involved in the actual murder.[38]

TRADEMARK IN CHARACTERS

The Snow White fiasco, mentioned earlier, along with many of the cases reviewed throughout this chapter, strongly suggests some de facto merger between copyright and trademark in protecting "Miss White" and her fictional colleagues. The language of relevant opinions often sounds more like the reasoning of trademark and unfair competition than that of copyright protection. Many times, both property rights can be asserted. In other cases, the matter turns on trademark and unfair competition.

In a case comparable to the one involving Amos and Andy but decided five years earlier in the Southern District of New York, Aquaman and his entourage were before the court. The case involved television characters being commercialized in the toy and game markets.[39] Since 1941 DC Comics had been publishing the Aquaman series. Among the characters were the woman Mera and a walrus type called Tusky and a villain, Black Manta. In the sixties, DC Comics contracted with ABC for an animated series and marketed corresponding toys and games. Similarly, Plastic Man was marketed in the sixties with an ABC television version broadcast in 1979.

In 1978 CBS began marketing its Manta and Moray and Supersleuth series. DC Comics raised a variety of claims, most significantly including trademark infringement. Defending itself under the Lanham Act, the defendant argued that the CBS characters were not designed to palm off the ABC counterparts and, therefore, no liability attached. The court held this to be too narrow a reading of trademark protection and refused to disturb the verdict for the plaintiffs. DC Comics fared no better in seeking actual destruction of the defendant's films and materials. Its argument that characters, including their traits and abilities, are protected was also rejected, as too broadly stated.

The court expanded on this point to hold as protectable names and nicknames of entertainment characters, their physical appearance, and their costumes. Not protected are their physical abilities and personality traits. In fact, the court asserted that there were no cases under the Lanham Act finding these characteristics protectable.

Similarly, The Fifth Circuit has held the name Conan the Barbarian to be a protectable trademark infringed by Conans Pizza.[40]

SYNTHESIS

The foregoing case law on the protection of fictional characters may best be synthesized with reference to a case in the Northern District of Georgia.[41] An action for a judgment declaring the conveyance of sequel rights in Margaret Mitchell's *Gone with the Wind* was before the court. Throughout the history of the distribution of the rights in the novel, sequel rights had either been left unmentioned or had expressly been retained by Margaret Mitchell and her successors.

That David O. Selznick, producer of *Gone with the Wind*, never considered the sequel rights to be his is manifest in his documented—but unsuccessful—efforts to secure them. Indeed, the author made it abundantly clear that she was reluctant to release Scarlett and Rhett and the others to anyone. She had created them and would fight to defend them against misuse or abuse by any other writer.[42] In fact, there had been a series of licensing agreements, entered in 1936, 1939, 1961, and 1975. The agreement of 1939, addressing "commercial tie-ups" expressly withheld conveyance of any literary right in the novel, its characters, or their names. It also withheld sequel rights, as well as those to condensation, adaptation, or " 'to describe or picture the characters in new situations, scenes or adventures' " including serials, comic strips, or caricatures.[43] In short, Scarlett and the others had expressly been preserved from the precise issue raised in the Sam Spade case. Similarly, the 1961 licensing agreement, addressing certain copyright renewal rights, preserved sequel rights with specific reference to the characters. It precluded any "production with the plot or the story or the characters . . . in which the lives of the characters . . . [are] carried beyond the time of the ending of the Novel."[44] The 1975 contract, on which the case ultimately depended, did contemplate a sequel, but the contractual prerequisites that would have transferred the rights to MGM/UA were never met.[45]

Hence, according to the licensing agreements, based on the copyright in the property, all sequel rights belonged to the plaintiff, Margaret Mitchell's successor, with particular reference to the characters—leaving nothing available to MGM/UA absent a new agreement. The matter of trademark entered the decision in that the defendant's last-ditch argument was to the effect that any new sequel arising out of the plaintiff's intellectual properties would harm ("dilute") its existing film property, Selznick's *Gone with the Wind*. The court simply held that the defendant had failed to meet its burden in establishing this possibility.

Obviously the controversial protection of characters, as such, is dependent on three aspects of the law: copyright, trademark, and contract. Copyright is the first line of defense, on which contractual distributions will ultimately depend, with the notable exception of the Ninth Circuit, which will enforce contractual distribution of character, express or construed, without yet recognizing the attendant property as copyright. But trademark, and its companion unfair competition, can afford additional protection, throughout the federal jurisdictions. These protections, going by any name, are especially crucial in the case of characters who have taken a strong hold on the public imagination.

To a certain extent, then, either contract law or trademark principles will serve to extend any copyright rights vested in fictional characters presented through the several media serving the popular arts. This intriguing aspect of applicable law will be addressed in some detail in the next two chapters. The working premise is the existence of copyright in characters, which will be explored in the final chapter.

NOTES

1. *See The Protection Afforded Literary and Cartoon Characters through Trademark, Unfair Competition, and Copyright*, 68 HARV. L. REV. 349 (1954) and Marks, *Legal Rights and Fictional Characters*, 25 COPYRIGHT L. SYMP. (ASCAP) 35 (1980). The latter provides an appendix listing articles which address the issues of character protection.

2. 17 U.S.C. 102.

3. 17 U.S.C. 106, 113.

4. 17 U.S.C. 501.

5. 2 M. NIMMER and D. NIMMER, NIMMER ON COPYRIGHT §2.12, at 2–171—2–178.2.

6. Personal communication with Mr. Morrell, Chicago, 1983.

7. *See* D. MORRELL, RAMBO/FIRST BLOOD PART II (1985).

8. Yankwich, *Originality in the Law of Intellectual Property (Its Meaning from a Legal and Literary Standpoint)*, 11 F.R.D. 457 (1952), at 466.

For a general review of copyright *see* W. STRONG, THE COPYRIGHT BOOK/A PRACTICAL GUIDE (2d ed. 1984).

9. Marks breaks character into three discrete elements for legal analysis: Name, physical appearance, and personality (which he equates with characterization). The character must then be "presented" in written words or in words and pictures. Marks, *supra* note 1, at 37–38.

10. Marks has asserted that this question only leads to confusion and misleading reasoning. *See supra* note 1, at 40. This commentator insists that the cases turn not on copyrightability but on infringement and alludes to potential confusion when the true issue of copyrightability itself arises. But note that without copyrightability in the first instance, infringement cannot arise.

11. Berman and Boxer, *Copyright Infringement of Audiovisual Works and Characters*, 52 S. CAL. L. REV. 315 (1979).

12. Ibid., at 324.

13. Ibid.

14. Ibid.

15. Ibid., at 330–331.

16. Hill v. Whalen & Martell, 220 F. 359 (S.D. N.Y. 1914).

17. 220 F. at 360.

18. Prouty v. National Broadcasting Co., 26 F. Supp. 265 (D. Mass. 1939).

19. 26 F. Supp. at 266.

20. Warner Bros. Pictures v. Columbia Broadcasting System, 216 F.2d 945 (9th Cir. 1954).

21. 216 F.2d at 950.

22. 216 F.2d at 951. (Citations omitted.)

23. W. STRONG, *supra* note 8, at 17.

24. *See, e.g.*, Turner, *Well, Nobody Ever Claimed She Had a Sense of Humor*, WALL ST. J. (April 3, 1989), at 1.

25. Stern v. United States, 164 F. Supp. 847 (E.D. La. 1958).

26. 164 F. Supp. at 852.

27. Warner Bros. v. Film Ventures International, 403 F. Supp. 522 (C.D. Cal. 1975).

28. 403 F. Supp. at 522.

29. Olson v. National Broadcasting Co., 855 F.2d 1446 (9th Cir. 1988).

30. 855 F.2d at 1451.

31. *See* chapters 6 and 7.

32. 855 F.2d at 1451.

33. Giangrasso v. CBS, 215 U.S.P.Q. 219 (E.D. N.Y. 1982).

34. 215 U.S.P.Q. at 223–224.

35. Filmvideo Releasing Corp. v. Hastings, 426 F. Supp. 690, 509 F. Supp. 60 (S.D. N.Y. 1981).

36. 426 F. Supp. 690 and 509 F. Supp. 60, *passim.*

37. Silverman v. CBS, 632 F. Supp. 1344 (S.D. N.Y. 1986), at 1355.

38. Rossner v. CBS, 612 F. Supp. 334 (S.D. N.Y. 1985).

39. DC Comics v. Filmation Associates, 486 F. Supp. 1273 (S.D. N.Y. 1980).

40. Conan Properties v. Conans Pizza, 752 F.2d 145 (5th Cir. 1985). (For reasons irrelevant to this discussion, the infringement was not enjoined.)

41. Trust Co. Bank v. MGM/UA Entertainment, 593 F. Supp. 580 (N.D. GA. 1984).

42. 593 F. Supp. at 583.

43. 593 F. Supp. at 584.

44. Ibid.

45. Ibid.

6

Special Characters, Special Cases

All the world loves a hero. He need not be mythic, but he is always larger than life. Today the hero is very much a part of popular culture. From the legal perspective, the hero as archetype is in the public domain; he is part of psychology's collective unconscious. By definition, everyone has access to him in one form or another. But when archetypal heroes are created for the popular arts they are properties—and extraordinarily valuable ones at that.

Heroes of the popular arts take on pecuniary value because they provide something special to their audiences. But, as was suggested in the case of *Star Wars* in chapter 3, this special relationship can actually interfere with management of the attendant intellectual property rights. The principal characters from *Star Wars*, most notably Luke Skywalker and Darth Vader, are powerful images that individual members of their immense audience assimilate for themselves. This taking can be a powerful force in assuring a healthy future for the properties, but it can also be dangerous to the proprietor of the characters. Under the law, a popular hero can be loved to death: the authors of the various intellectual properties risk loss of artistic control and inevitable lapse of the character into the public domain.

In this chapter and the next, fictional characters who have "lived long and prospered" because of their grip on the public imagination will be examined in the light of copyright and trademark property. Because they are types arising out of the Western mythos, the unique features of each will be placed in the tradition of his intellectual origins.

In preparation for review of the relevant case law, the legal management of each character will be considered. Thus, the interplay among intellectual history, the law of copyright and trademark, and contractual distributions of properties will be illustrated. In this chapter, two heroes of America's old West and one who represents a blending of science fiction with fantasy will be studied. The chapter concludes with a particularly successful ensemble out of the science fiction genre.

The Lone Ranger and Superman are each representative of a successful intellectual venture coupled with successful legal protection of the resultant properties. The strange saga of Paladin reveals how the legal system can fail an author when another takes possession of his creation and transforms it into a popular phenomenon. Captain Kirk, Mr. Spock, and the crew of the Star Ship Enterprise represent what may be a unique, but extraordinarily successful, approach to building characters in cooperation with the consuming public while retaining control over the properties.

In chapter 7, the extraordinary history of Edgar Rice Burroughs's most gripping character, Tarzan of the Apes, will be detailed. Here is the character who comes closest to being an archetype in and of himself. Tarzan's phenomenal popularity was nearly instantaneous and has survived more than fifty years, albeit envisioned in multiple forms—perhaps as many as there are members of his vast audience. Among contemporary heroes of popular culture, Tarzan is the only one who may be destined for the lofty pinnacle of the literary classic.

Equally extraordinary are the heroic efforts of Tarzan's creator (and his successor, Edgar Rice Burroughs, Inc.) to maintain control of the phenomenon that is Tarzan. The chronicle of relevant cases provides an invaluable model of the array of legal mechanisms protecting fictional characters.

THE LONE RANGER

Lone Ranger Television, Inc., a subsidiary of Wrather Corporation, is the owner of all rights, title, and interest in and to the Lone Ranger property, including but not limited to all copyrights and trademarks pertaining thereto, all Lone Ranger radio programs, and recordings thereof, all motion pictures and television programs, all publications, comic strips and comic books, and all rights to commercial usage of the names and images of the characters and all other related identifications of the property.

Permission has been granted the author by Lone Ranger Television, Inc. for the inclusion of certain pictorial and literary material in this book, which material is protected by its copyrights in and to the Lone Ranger property. Such permission does not convey any interest in the material to the author, publisher, or any other person or firm.[1]

Such are the lengths to which creators and proprietors of literary works chronicling the exploits of popular fictional characters must go to protect those properties from their artistic colleagues and fans alike. As will become readily apparent, the first line of legal defense is the cautious and precise drafting of licensing agreements. The second line of defense is the tough posture reflected in the language quoted above. The last resort is the courts, to assert copyright or trademark infringement.

Intellectual Origins; Copyrightability

When he was created for radio in 1933, the Long Ranger was conceived of as a benevolent outlaw. Creator George W. Trendle's prototypes were Robin Hood and Zorro and certain characters among the writings of Zane Grey, James Fenimore Cooper, and Horatio Alger. Perhaps the Ranger had been unjustly banished and was waiting to come back into his own, because he was basically decent and athletic in addition to being alert and enterprising.[2] Because he was to be a former

Texas Ranger, this character would be known as the Lone Ranger.

It was Fran Striker who developed the story establishing this hero. Striker saw the Lone Ranger as tall and slim. The author provided his emerging hero with the now famous silver hallmarks—silver bullets and silver shoes and the name "Silver" for his horse, which had to be white. The creative process occurred over some time before the trial radio show was aired.[3]

As the show progressed the masked man's somber personality began to emerge. Initially he had been too cheerful. Lightness was inappropriate for a masked avenger. His mission of righting wrongs, protecting the poor and weak, and bringing peace and justice to the frontier was hardly a laughing matter. After some ten broadcasts, Tonto was introduced because this was radio and the hero needed a companion to whom he could talk, describing events.[4]

Actually, a number of individuals contributed to this creative process. And, in fact, Fran Striker was not to establish the history of the Lone Ranger's origins until the radio show had been running for a number of years. It was this history that explained the background of the mask and the use of silver. Thereafter the characters continued to evolve, especially through their television portrayals.[5]

Originally, *The Lone Ranger* was heard only in Michigan, but by 1939 it was carried on 140 stations in the United States and elsewhere and produced an income of $500,000 a year. "No other fictional broadcasting character remained so popular for so long and made so much money for its owners."[6]

The money was one thing, but even more significant was "what the character came to mean to his millions of listeners, viewers and readers throughout the years."[7] As has happened with many other highly popular characters, the Lone Ranger approached a kind of reality through his creators—writers, producers, directors, actors—and perhaps even more significantly through the imaginations of those who listened and later listened and watched. An aura eventually surrounded the character beyond anything the creators could have accomplished.[8]

A stirring fictional character must always be given a uniquely personal aura within the imagination of each reader or viewer, but when a character is very popular that aura begins to assume some degree of independently created "reality" that may belong more to the fans than to the proprietors. Such possession by the fans cannot usurp that of the legally recognized proprietors unless they "sleep on their rights," but time and again it has proven to be a potent force nonetheless.

The early proprietors of the Lone Ranger, who were also his creators, recognized a need for consistency in his presentation. Thus, they must have been literary pioneers in establishing rules to be followed by those writing the episodes. Further, a writers' guide was prepared, no doubt among the forerunners to Star Trek's guide, written some twenty years in the future. Not only does this early guide establish limits on the type of material considered appropriate, it reemphasizes the nature of the character, with more than one caveat regarding that unique personal aura each imagination creates.[9]

In addition to the live radio show, which ended in 1954, there were television incarnations, including cartoons and the inevitable syndications, and the film versions of the thirties, the fifties and the eighties. There was also a little-known stage presentation. This one-act play was an "added attraction" to accompany a feature film.[10]

Throughout the years, numerous actors have assumed the mask and the persona of the Lone Ranger. The first, Earl Graser, died suddenly and left the producers with a problem to be resolved with considerable ingenuity. The artists knew that the sudden shock of a new voice for the Lone Ranger would be disruptive for the listening audience and carried the potential for long-term harm. The eventual decision was that the Lone Ranger be seriously wounded and unable to speak for a couple of weeks. Tonto would carry the program. Then, for a while, the hero would speak in only a whisper. Gradually his "full, rich" voice would return.[11] The new voice was that of the unforgettable Brace Beemer, the most famous Lone Ranger of them all. Just as Johnny Weissmuller took on the persona of Tarzan, Beemer became the quintessence of the Lone Ranger.[12]

With Beemer, the point of demarcation between the character and the actor's personification of it was not readily discerned by the actor or by observers. Some observers noted that

Beemer believed strongly in the ideals of the Lone Ranger but never accepted the spontaneous public response as his due.[13] Like Tarzan and so many other heroes of popular literary properties, the Lone Ranger came to stand for something special. In the case of the masked man, this feature of the character was acknowledged and respected by those in artistic control.[14]

The year 1949 marked the television premiere of *The Lone Ranger*, making the character a pioneer of this medium. The integrity of the initial characterization was sustained, and the chosen actors personified mental images of the radio audience. Carefully designed and tailored costuming served to complete the desired image.[15]

For the first episodes Clayton Moore was the Lone Ranger. After another actor took over for a while, Moore returned.[16] Certainly he has become identified with the character at least to the same extent as Brace Beemer before him. But, when the nostalgia craze of the late seventies struck, Moore was "eased" out of the role. (Jay Silverheels, the best-known Tonto, was already in poor health and died in 1980.) In 1977 *Variety* ran an advertisement announcing plans for the film, *The Legend of the Lone Ranger*.[17]

After the midthirties, newspaper comic strips and comic books were in production subject to licensing agreements. Dell's monthly comic book closely followed the radio adventures. But the appearance of the Lone Ranger altered over time in conformance with changes in the popular image of cowboy heroes.[18]

From 1936 through 1957 Fran Striker wrote eighteen novels, originally published by Grossett & Dunlap. The novels are reportedly well written and in the radio tradition. Not surprisingly, they present the most complete view of the character. In this format the characters and plot could be fully developed.[19]

Legal Management; Copyright, Trademark, and Licensing

George W. Trendle actually received sole credit for the creation of the Lone Ranger. He oversaw both the writing and the production of the radio series and assigned a production coordinator to maintain the integrity of the character on television.

Trendle is charged with only one lapse, connected to his dealings with Republic Studios: despite a reputation for business acumen and protectiveness, Trendle permitted Republic to produce two serials without any stipulation for consistency with the radio material.[20]

As a result, the 1938 and 1939 serials bore little resemblance to their source. Even the Ranger's name was changed more than once, and his identity was known to the audience. Consequently Trendle withheld the Lone Ranger from cinema production for some ten years and retained artistic control over television production.[21]

The Lone Ranger, Incorporated was organized in 1935. In the midfifties Trendle sold this intellectual property to Jack Wrather for $3 million. Copyrights in Striker's novels are held by Lone Ranger Television, Inc., a subsidiary of Wrather Corporation.[22]

In part, the integrity of the properties was maintained by retention of actual production. The sponsor, General Mills, paid the bills but had no say about casting, writing, or directing. Further, the director was instructed to work closely with Striker. Under the control of Wrather, color features were made in 1955 and 1958, the earlier grossing more than $1.5 million.

The Cases; Trademark and Unfair Competition

The earliest reported pirating of the Lone Ranger dates from 1940.[23] In the next year, a second case was reported.[24] Actor Lee Powell had portrayed "Allen King," a character unmasked as the Lone Ranger in a 15–episode serial released in 1940 as a feature. Now the actor was appearing with the Cox Circus, billed as the original Lone Ranger. The resultant suit was based in unfair competition. It was not successful: there was no infringement of copyright and relief on the trademark issue was denied. According to the court, Powell was not passing himself off as the Lone Ranger because he had played the role.

The Lone Ranger, Inc., no less intrepid than its namesake, did not give up. The matter was taken to the circuit court of appeals.[25] The sole theory on appeal was unfair competition. The appellate court reversed the trial court's recognition of the actor's claim to a right to use the fact of his first appearance as the Lone Ranger. The appellate court held that the defendants' claim was calculated to attract the plaintiffs' audience and did therefore constitute passing off.

But the matter was hardly laid to rest.[26] In the next case, the defendant, Earl W. Currey, billed himself repeatedly as being en route to Hollywood with his famous horse Silver. Currey first used the Lone Ranger identity in early 1940 in Houston, to the confusion of the press, but the releases were corrected upon the plaintiff's reaction. It happened again in 1947, but, no doubt, the last straw was added when Currey so unmercifully beat his horse during an appearance that the Humane Society became involved. The plaintiff was obliged to take out ads denying any connection to Currey.

With a detailed recognition of the Lone Ranger and his fictional world, the court found a pattern of falsehood and concluded that the Lone Ranger, having acquired secondary meaning, was entitled to protection. An injunction was in order because of the irreparable damage that would follow from the defendant's cheating, fraud, and deceit.[27]

A related, but far more difficult situation began to emerge as early as the sixties, although it has only recently been resolved—without fanfare. In the sixties, Clayton Moore was making personal appearances as the Lone Ranger. Although these appearances frequently grossed more than $100,000 a year, proprietor Wrather demanded no compensation. Significantly, Moore was helping to keep the character before the public at a time when westerns were out of favor.[28] Circumstances altered substantially in the seventies. After Moore was "eased out" of the role, the public accepted replacements in advertisements and in Macy's Thanksgiving parade. But, in the spring of 1978, Moore sued Wrather, alleging exploitation and the wrongful deprivation of Moore's "likeness, voice and actual photographs and movie clips." (The label, "right of publicity," was not reported.) The actor dismissed his case with prejudice later in the same year. Moore continued with his personal appearances.[29]

Meanwhile the planned Lone Ranger film was delayed because of script difficulties. More than two years passed before filming could commence. As the preparations moved into casting, it must have become apparent that the Clayton Moore situation had become untenable. Suit for injunction was filed in August 1979, and a preliminary injunction was issued by the end of the month despite the inundation of letters on Moore's behalf.[30]

In the end Wrather allowed the appearances to continue but without the mask, because with the mask Moore *became the Lone Ranger*. Moore actually switched to sunglasses and rather forlornly voiced a hope that the producers would continue to live up to the moral code he had kept alive.[31]

But the public was outraged on Moore's behalf. Moore's plight caught the fancy of the general public beyond the expectations of Wrather. Petitions for the return of the mask were circulated widely. There was even talk of a boycott of Wrather productions, particularly the upcoming film.[32]

Other than putatively sincere written responses to inquiries, the Lone Ranger Corporation could do little more than maintain a discreet silence. Whether the attendant publicity helped or hurt the new film—and any future incarnations of the Lone Ranger—only the proprietors can know for certain. The mask of office ultimately was quietly restored to Clayton Moore. To most living fans, *he is* the masked man. Thus is illustrated the mixture of need and hazard presented by the die-hard fans of a popular character. Long-lived popularity depends on them, but control of the character can be lost to—or through—them.

SUPERMAN

Intellectual Origins; Copyrightability

Created by Jerry Siegel and Joseph Shuster for Action Comics, the initial Superman story appeared in June of 1938.[33] By 1939 there was a daily comic strip in addition to the comic book.[34] Superman made his radio debut in February of 1940.[35] Already changes in the character had commenced. Originally conceived of as a man able to hurdle skyscrapers and to leap something less than a mile, Superman was soon literally flying. His strength also increased as did his speed. Although he began by outracing a train, Superman was exceeding the speed of light and traveling through time by the late forties. His invulnerability also grew. In 1939 Superman was not quite immune to a bursting shell, but with the advent of the Second World War he was shrugging them off. At the close of the war he could survive atomic blasts.[36]

Superman started without super senses. Then, in one story, he suspected a man he was seeking was in a certain house. In order to find the man, Superman had to crash through the roof. X-ray vision was a useful expedient. The dual identity was initially contrived because Superman was wanted by the police for taking the law into his own hands. Despite this shaky beginning, however, Superman eventually began working with the police.[37]

In addition to appearing in the comics, Superman appeared in nearly twenty color cartoons with full animation intended to challenge Disney in style and brilliance. In 1948 and 1950 two serials were produced by Columbia, and in 1951 George Reeves starred in *Superman and the Mole Men*. The live-action television series ran from 1951 to 1957. In the midseventies there were eight comic books being published in thirty countries in fifteen different languages.[38]

In fact, it was partly the multiplicity of media in which Superman was appearing that dictated the changes in him. In 1942 the first novel (entitled *Superman*) by George Lowther appeared. Originally an advanced Terran, Superman became an alien from Krypton. His powers then could be explained as a consequence of the physical differences in the two planets.[39] Over the years Superman continued to exert a universal appeal, which was reactivated in the late seventies through an updating retelling of his origins.[40] In fact, when the television show ceased production, Superman's renown increased rather than diminished, and the show remained among the most popular reruns.[41] There has even been a Broadway musical: *It's a Bird . . . It's a Plane . . . It's Superman.*[42]

It was the radio show, however, that came up with many innovations that may explain something of Superman's longevity. That which most changed the growing Superman legend was Kryptonite, in its several forms—all of them hazardous to Superman's health, physical or mental. In 1948 personal touches began to be added to the Superman saga, most notably the introduction of Lois Lane. The source of his powers were made clearer. Then Lana Lang was added to the retinue. But marriage was expressly out of the question because Superman's career would jeopardize his wife.[43]

Superman's alter ego is an interesting study in and of himself. In a 1940 comic strip Clark Kent is described as meek, but in 1971 he is advanced to being a television reporter for the Galaxy Broadcasting System,[44] described as "a savvy and stylish television newscaster with natty European-cut clothing in the best tradition of hip investigative reporters."[45]

Legal Management; Copyright, Trademark, and Licensing

There are no reports to indicate that his fans have threatened to exert control over the destiny of Superman—perhaps because until recently there has been no single incarnation (in written or human form) that has captivated popular imagination. The Superman epic seems to be popular on a level different from that of Tarzan or the Lone Ranger or the *Star Trek* ensemble. Nevertheless, numerous cases in point have been reported, and Warner Bros. was contractually bound to preserve the integrity of the character, which they did to a surprising degree.[46]

It took Superman's original creators years to put him into commercial publication despite their marketing efforts. The writer, Jerry Siegel, was inspired by fantasy in general and by Lester Dent's *Doc Savage* and Philip Wylie's 1932 *Gladiator* in particular.[47] It is worth noting at this juncture that the actual creators of the Superman epic are not the authors of the associated intellectual properties.[48] Siegel and Shuster transferred all rights to Superman to Detective Comics (predecessor to National Periodical Publications) through a series of employment contracts entered in the forties. Although the artists were relatively well remunerated for their creation, the transfer of all rights must have lost them millions of dollars by now. The transfer of rights was legally validated in the late forties, and thirty years later the validation was deemed *res judicata* for purposes of copyright renewal rights.[49]

The Cases

Copyright. It was not long before the first imitator of Superman was brought to court.[50] The imitator was Wonderman, who was found to be altogether too similar to Superman: each wore ordinary clothing to conceal his strength. Both wore skin-tight "acrobatic" costumes when active—one blue and one red. They were both champions of the oppressed and engaged in a list of comparable stunts, including stopping bullets in mid-flight and leaping over or between buildings. "Each is described as the strongest man in the world and each as battling against 'evil and injustice.' "[51]

Not surprisingly, the defendants argued that the attributes of both characters are to be found in literature and mythology, but the court would have none of it. Although the two works were quite obviously deemed trivial, the court could hardly dismiss them. Together the works were found to

> embody an original arrangement of incidents and a pictorial and literary form which preclude the contention that [defendant] was not copying the antics of "Superman" portrayed [by plaintiffs]. We think it plain that the defendants have used more than general types and ideas and have appropriated the pictorial and literary details embodied in the . . . copyrights.[52]

Moreover, the court added, the matter of prior literature is relevant only to the question of source; specifically, whether that source is prior art or the complaining author's work. Here, the source was found to be the Superman work, which was subject to copyright and, hence, infringement was found at least to the extent that "the pictorial representations and verbal descriptions of 'Superman' are not a mere delineation of a benevolent Hercules, but embody an arrangement of incidents and literary expressions original with the authors."[53]

In finding infringement, however, the Second Circuit modified the injunction issued by the trial court to narrow it to only those materials "portraying the feats of strength or powers performed by 'Superman' or closely imitating his costume or appearance."[54] No one, according to the appellate court, is entitled to a monopoly on some "superman" who is a blessing to society.

The next case asked whether certain Superman comic strips at issue had been subject to proper copyright notice.[55] Later the question of abandonment of copyright in Superman comic strips was raised.[56] This time Fawcett's Captain Marvel had been found to infringe on Superman. The issue arose because the publisher of the Superman strip had neglected the requisite copyright formalities. Had the holder of the copyright thereby abandoned all rights to the pictorial portrayals of Superman's exploits?

The court accepted that the particular strips published without copyright notice were in the public domain but went on to hold that such lapse affected no other strip. So complete a loss could only occur in the event the lapses were so frequent as to justify the inference of abandonment with reference to future works.

Trademark. The related unfair competition (analogous to trademark) action was held by the court to be baseless, with some words to the wise for potential infringers:

> The owner's right to protect his name or mark . . . depends primarily upon the likelihood that those who may wish to deal with him will be misled into dealing with the infringer; and that presupposes, not only that the mark has become associated with the owner as the source of the goods, but that this association is an inducement to deal with the owner. In the case of these silly pictures nobody cares who is the producer—least of all, children who are the chief readers—; the "strips" sell because they amuse and please, and they amuse and please because they are what they are, not because they come from "Detective." To allow the first producer of such pictures to prevent others from copying them, save as he can invoke the Copyright Law, would sanction a completely indefensible monopoly.[57]

Later in the fifties the trademark issue was held in a slightly different light. National Comics opposed the registration of Superman as a trademark for bread.[58] Upon appeal of the holding that there was no claim upon which relief could be granted, the Commissioner of Patents ordered that the opposition be heard—implying the possible existence of a trademark in some aspect of Superman, most likely the name itself.

By the seventies trademark was very much in the fore. Unfair competition and dilution in violation of the Lanham Act were asserted against publishers of a periodical entitled *Daily Planet*.[59] Appropriately enough, the action arose in Metropolis itself: New York City.

According to the district court, the original *Daily Planet* serves two purposes in the existence of the Superman character. It is primarily the name of the fictitious newspaper which employs Superman's alter ego along with other principal characters. But "Daily Planet" is also the title of a promotional news column appearing within Superman comic books.[60]

The defendant's publication was of "underground news" and had been dormant from 1969 through 1973. Notably, with both parties claiming exclusive rights, the defendant's timing coincided with the scheduled release of the multimillion dollar film production.[61]

The court held that the issue was whether either party was entitled to exclusive exploitation of the name "based on the expected wave of public interest in the Superman character calculated to result from the release of the Superman movie."[62] Since neither had registered the mark, common law of trademark was to be applied. To make a case in New York, the common law claimant must demonstrate secondary meaning; namely, identification of producer rather than product in the consuming public. The essential elements of trademark infringement were reviewed, with an undeniable emphasis on character and acknowledgement of merchandising potential.[63]

Ultimately, the court found that the defendants had abandoned their mark, while "it is apparent that . . . plaintiff has demonstrated an association of such duration and consistency with the Daily Planet sufficient to establish a common law trademark therein. The . . . evidence demonstrates that the Daily Planet has over the years become inextricably woven into the fabric of the Superman story."[64] In the end, the defendants' motion was denied, and the plaintiff was granted a preliminary injunction.

The parody defense to copyright infringement. Once Warner Bros. secured certain rights in Superman, it, too, went about challenging unfair competition and copyright infringement. One seemingly unlikely target was ABC's *The Greatest American Hero.*[65] This time the Second Circuit took due note of Superman's remarkable commercial success over the span of more than forty years and of his fictional biography as recalled in the recent film extravaganza.

The main character of ABC's series, Ralph Hinkley, was by way of contrast an ordinary type whose extraordinary powers had been bestowed upon him along with a costume and an instruction book. Sadly, the latter had been lost. To say that this particular hero was inept is to put it kindly. The court saw little legally significant resemblance between Ralph and Superman and indulged in some wry comparisons.[66]

Given Hinkley's shortcomings, the lower court had rejected the copyright claim for lack of substantial similarity. Appeal was taken on the contention of improper focus on differences rather than on substantial similarities. Without using the terms *scènes à faire* or *parody* the Second Circuit acknowledged shared ideas, themes, and general imagery but found them insufficiently particular or concrete to constitute an appropriation of expression. The district court's focus on differences was held to be proper. Thus, the denial of preliminary injunction was affirmed.

Permanent injunction was then denied through the defendants' motion for summary judgment—based in copyright principles, Lanham Act provisions, and unfair competition.[67] The district court held, as a matter of law, that the premiere and seven episodes of *The Greatest American Hero* were not substantially similar to the two recent *Superman* movies, three television shows, and some twenty comic books.

Upon viewing *Superman II* and seven episodes of Ralph Hinkley's exploits, the court found "that what defendants took from plaintiffs' works and incorporated into TGAH were unprotected ideas."[68] The phenomenal abilities at issue are all nonhuman, but are attributes that people have long desired. The ability to fly is a prime example. The court noted that it "is neither concrete enough to be protected nor original to plaintiffs. It is also a prime example of a power which Hinkley never masters."[69] As for superbreath, the court observed that it was popularized as early as the *Three Little Pigs*.

It is worth noting in passing, as did the court, that case law in the Second Circuit does recognize protection of characters independent of the written, copyrighted context of their existence. But, according to this circuit, character as originally conceived and presented must be sufficiently developed to command such protection, and the alleged infringer must copy *that development*. With regard to Superman, the court said:

> As he is displayed in pictures in comic books, and by actors in the television and movie works, Superman is more readily protectable than he would be had he been merely a word portrait. . . .
>
> After forty years of development in various media, Superman is a well-defined character sufficiently developed to deserve copyright protection.[70]

From that important point of departure, numerous distinctions in the two characters were specified.

In addressing the elements of the Lanham Act claims, this court simply presumed the requisite secondary meaning in "phrases and other indicia used by plaintiffs for the character. Thus, the phrase 'it's a bird, it's a plane, it's Superman' has secondary meaning as does the specific Superman costume. The court [did] not find, however, that plaintiffs have the right to claim secondary meaning and protection for ideas."[71]

Next, the court found confusion of the sources of the two characters to be unlikely: "Superman is 'faster than a speeding bullet, more powerful than a locomotive, able to leap tall buildings in a single bound.' " Ralph Hinkley, on the other hand " 'may be unable to leap tall buildings in a single bound,. . . may be slower than a speeding bullet, and . . . may be less powerful than a locomotive . . . [but] he's just getting started.' "[72] In any event the respective contexts of these two phrases reflect the "vast difference" in the "total concept and feel" of the two.

PALADIN

Intellectual Origins; Protectability

In the late forties a mechanic from Cranston, Rhode Island, dressed up in a black cowboy outfit. There was a medal in his black hat and the image of a chess knight on his holster. Under his arm was concealed an antique derringer. At parades and similar events this "Paladin" rode his horse and handed out business cards emblazoned with the same chess device and with the legend "Have Gun Will Travel, Wire Paladin," followed by his Rhode Island address.[73]

Sound familiar? It should: From the late fifties into the sixties CBS ran the television show, *Have Gun Will Travel*. Enormously popular over its eight-year run, the show earned some $14 million.

CBS claimed spontaneous generation when the mechanic, Victor DeCosta, filed suit in the latter half of the sixties. At trial, DeCosta may have enjoyed the satisfaction of proving to a jury that CBS and the rest of the defendants were pirates, but he enjoyed little else for his trouble. The appellate court reversed verdicts totalling some $150,000. DeCosta, the court averred, was entitled to no share in the profits.[74]

Legal Management and Cases

The action had been brought under Rhode Island law, and the specific count at issue dealt with copyright protection. The upshot of the First Circuit's opinion rejecting the claim is that Congress could have provided for protection of characters, but that such creations are too slight to warrant it.[75] Heaping insult upon injury, the appellate court added that DeCosta's performance of Paladin was an unprotectable idea and that, while his cards were writings, they were not copyrightable.

The inevitable inference from this decision is that intellectual piracy is acceptable under the law so long as the pirate is big enough—one can only surmise the result had DeCosta's Paladin followed that of Richard Boone. What bears repeating in this context is that, not only is there a difference in plagiarism and infringement, there is also a distinction to be drawn between moral and legal wrongs. Again, only the latter are cognizable in the courtroom.

But DeCosta was obviously not one to give up easily. In 1962 he applied for registration of the phrase "Have Gun Will Travel," the knight device and the name Paladin as entertainment services.[76] CBS promptly opposed the registration, filing as a prior user. Unfortunately, a default judgment was entered in 1964, and DeCosta did not seek to set it aside until 1969. Although DeCosta argued problems with his legal counsel, the Appeal Board held the five-year delay to be inexcusable negligence. The default judgment went undisturbed.

Then in 1974 a small headline in the *Chicago Tribune* proclaimed, "CBS 'pirated' Paladin: judge."[77] The headline reflected DeCosta's victory on trial on remand to the federal district court. But attorneys for CBS vowed an appeal, asserting that the writers of the show had created Paladin in California and had never even been in New England where DeCosta had been appearing in horse shows and rodeos since 1946. Nearly a decade later, it was all over. And DeCosta had finally lost the legal battle, despite winning its moral counterpart yet again. The initial action, having been remanded to the district court, had been tried. DeCosta had won, and CBS had appealed, just as its lawyers had promised.

DeCosta had sought recovery for the unauthorized use of his character concept, composed of the costume, slogan, name, and symbols. His argument was based in Rhode Island's common law trademark (or, here, service mark) and unfair competition. By consent of the parties, the matter was referred to a magistrate for findings of fact. The magistrate, however, in finding for DeCosta had entered findings of mixed fact and law. The latter went beyond the parties' consent. Hence the appeal.

After resolving the associated preliminary issues, the First Circuit went to the merits of the case. In reversing the judgment for DeCosta and remanding with instructions to enter judgment for CBS, the court's basic ruling was that, even conceding that the plaintiff's marks met the standards for common law service marks and were so distinctive as to obviate the need for proof of secondary meaning, the testimony of a handful of witnesses who believed the television character to have been DeCosta was insufficient evidence of confusion. The ruling in some part also acknowledged that DeCosta's activities had been restricted to New England and that he had waited eleven years before suing.[78] Taken together it all meant defeat.

DeCosta contended that the combination of the costume, knight, and the words *wire Paladin* constituted a distinctive mark for common law purposes. Further, the defendants had intentionally infringed it, appropriating the plaintiff's goodwill to his serious financial damage. DeCosta's second contention was that the defendants, in intentionally copying his marks and manner of dress, had passed the character off as the original and thereby profited while diluting the plaintiff's established goodwill. DeCosta was seeking injunctive relief and an accounting of defendants' profits. Then he sought a trebling of his lost profits and of damages he suffered plus $2 million in unspecified damages.

Addressing the trademark contention, the magistrate had found secondary meaning through twenty-one witnesses who had observed the original in character. Through those witnesses, six of whom had believed television's Paladin to be the Rhode Island original, the magistrate had found confusion. Finally, he had found commercial activity in DeCosta's activities.

With regard to the contention of unfair competition, the magistrate had found the prerequisite unavailability of copyright protection (which would have preempted application of state law). He had then found DeCosta's performances to be in interstate commerce and endowed with secondary meaning. While the two Paladins were not in direct competition, he had found that the defendants had infringed in falsely advertising Paladin as their own and, therefore, had engaged in unfair competition.

The appellate court observed, however, that two crucial allegations had not been adequately addressed in the magistrate's reasoning. They were financial damages in the trademark allegation and passing off in that of unfair competition. In fact, DeCosta's appearances were uncompensated, negating any allegation of financial damage. The appellate court also held that the defendants did not "draw luster from the [DeCosta] paradigm."[79] Indeed, this court asserted that the plaintiff could not have been found to be engaged in remunerative business sparked by the profit motive. To eliminate that essential element would be to establish an improper precedent.

It is, then, essential that a plaintiff alleging infringement of common law trademark be in a trade, business, or profession having goodwill to protect. People must be willing to pay for the service. On the other hand, if nonprofit, there must be sufficient investment to warrant protection.

For the sake of argument, the First Circuit was willing to assume these prerequisites in order to reach the major issue: deception of the public. Without a finding of passing off, the only remaining theory is confusion. But the plaintiff had not availed himself of the opportunity to supplement the record on this point and was already derelict in timely pursuit of his claim and, therefore, subject to laches. In the end all these factors combined to defeat DeCosta's legal position. The First Circuit had this to say as a last word:

> We recognize that plaintiff has lost something of value to him. The very success of defendants' series saturated the public consciousness and in time diluted the attractiveness of plaintiff's creation, although he continued his appearances longer than defendants' first run. While he was not injured financially, there can be no doubt that he has felt deprived. As a commentator has observed, "[I]t could be argued that the most appropriate measure of damages would be the emotional harm that he suffered when CBS exploited his character and lured his audience away." ... But to give any relief, however tailored, we need a predicate of liability. Absent the ultimate fact of confusion, we cannot find a basis for liability for common law service mark infringement or unfair competition.[80]

THE CREW OF THE STARSHIP ENTERPRISE

The year is 1988. The name of the novel is simply *Spock's World*. No more is needed for the potential buyer, but over the title are the words *Star Trek*. The brochure of the Science Fiction Book Club describes the book's contents, and—unique among the entries—the description is followed not solely by a copyright notice but also by the caveat that Star Trek is a registered trademark of Paramount Picture Corporation.[81]

The Making of Star Trek was written before the show's third season was aired.[82] It reflects the very beginning of a truly unique phenomenon among popular intellectual properties. Fandom has played a major *creative* role in the evolution of the crew of the Enterprise.

The original *Star Trek* has inspired a body of amateur literature that has been actively encouraged by the originators of the literary property. There is no measure to determine the degree to which those amateur efforts have served to keep Star Trek alive through no less than five theatrical films, a seemingly endless supply of pastiches, and the syndicated live-action *Star Trek: The New Generation*, the most recent television entry.

While it can be said that science fiction as a genre came into its own during the first half of the twentieth century, its place in the visual media lagged until the advent of *Star Trek* in the midsixties. The series marked the first time one of the major television networks accepted a premise beyond the standard horror of "bug-eyed monsters." *Star Trek* involved a substantial creative effort to establish a visual reality representing the future. That the effort succeeded cannot be doubted. It commanded a well-educated audience that has proven to be both articulate and literate.[83]

Producer-creator Gene Roddenberry insisted that *Star Trek* be legitimate science fiction, not fantasy. Further he insisted that science fiction is not a separate branch of literature. To him there is but a single body of literature, and characters are the binding agent. Moreover, *Star Trek* took the path of the better science fiction tradition. The artists provided a highly detailed background development for the show, but virtually none of it was explained to the viewer unless absolutely essential to the story.[84]

Whatever its literary strengths and whatever the explanation for *Star Trek*'s grip on the public's imagination, it survived two seasons but went into its third only after a major public outcry. The *Star Trek* phenomenon had started early but grew slowly. After those first two seasons, the show was in imminent danger of cancellation. If the television executives thought only the scientific elite watched *Star Trek*, they were quickly disabused of that notion by an enormous ground swell of protest, articulate as well as passionate. In March of 1968 NBC broke with television precedent to announce renewal on the air.[85]

By 1975 *Star Trek*'s fandom was "full-blown" and "fast growing."[86] In fact "Trekkies" outnumbered more traditional science fiction fans. Book sales were most revealing. If the typical sale of a science-fiction title was 40,000, that of a paperback novelization of *Star Trek* episodes was closer to 400,000. The eleven James Blish paperbacks had sold close to four million copies.[87] Fandom was obviously hungry for more.

Among the "professional products" were the eleven novelization anthologies, three works of nonfiction, the animated television series, and novelizations of the animated series. It was not enough. Star Trek fandom persisted in creating universes of their own.[88] Unlike other fan-created universes, theirs saw the light of commercial publication.[89] From fan-created universes have emerged a whole series of original novels continuing the *Star Trek* saga.

There can be no doubt that Roddenberry and his associates were astute enough to recognize that the unique quality of fan support for *Star Trek* was invaluable in the continued success of the voyages. But they have also been wise enough to take the requisite legal steps to ensure protection of the array of associated intellectual properties. A crucial part of this unique melding of proprietor and consuming public culminating in a quarter-century phenomenon is the quality of fandom.[90] In short, *Star Trek*'s fans actually represented something of an experimental industry. And this novel industry expanded while nurturing the original property following its seeming demise, "because STAR TREK, unlike a novel or series of novels, was not created by one person, and thus was not a kind of closed creation."[91]

In fact, the only reported case involving *Star Trek* as intellectual property arises from the unauthorized sale of videotapes.[92] The defense to the several theories advanced was lack of copyright notice. The matter turned on the legal definition of publication and the related distinction between general and limited publication, with specific reference to syndication. The court looked to the licensing agreements and found the publications limited (thus, in favor of Paramount) in that all the agreements provided that broadcast was only to nonpaying audiences, the licensee was not to part with possession of the tapes, no copies were to be made, and the tapes were to be returned.

No work in the popular media can take such a mighty grip on the imagination without something special in its makeup. In the case of *Star Trek*, it is the characterization and interaction among the bridge crew that are special.[93]

It was no accident. Scripts were on assignment only. Some thirty unsolicited manuscripts received from agents per month were returned (through attorneys).[94] Because of the matter-of-fact manner in which science was treated in the program, the scripts could emphasize the characters, making the overall effect amazingly real. Just how real was conveyed in a letter to Roddenberry from Leonard Nimoy following the actor's visit to NASA's Goddard Space Flight Center:

> "I do not overstate the fact when I tell you... it would almost seem they feel we are a dramatization of the future of their space program, and they have completely taken us to heart—particularly since... the production staff... have taken such great pains in the area of scientific detail.... They are, in fact, proud of the show as though in some way it represents them."[95]

Continuity in the show was also provided by that "family" of characters. Of them Mr. Spock stood out from the beginning, not always to the best advantage. The first pilot had been rejected, not only as too cerebral but also because of the alien presence. That Mr. Spock is of the same lineage that spawned Tarzan of the Apes is immediately apparent in Roddenberry's response to this initial reaction to Spock. " 'My own idea... was, in a very real sense, we are all aliens on a strange planet. We spend most of our lives reaching out and trying to communicate.... [A]nd this is exactly what Spock is trying to do.' "[96] Obviously, this brief statement goes far in explaining the lure of Tarzan and his kin, including Spock. With Spock there is the added feature of the hint of evil, to be compared with Tarzan's untamed savagery.[97] If any one aspect is to be singled out as the sole impetus to *Star Trek*'s longevity, that aspect has to be Mr. Spock. And his creation was not without calculation.

For example, the intended warmth between Kirk and Spock existed before the second series of pilots was established. Even then Spock's dual nature was already emerging. Spock is one of the only two people with whom Kirk can unbend. In Spock's case the friendship is based upon logic, high mutual respect, and Vulcan loyalty to a commander. With that seemingly humble beginning television history was in fact being made.[98]

NOTES

1. D. ROTHEL, WHO WAS THAT MASKED MAN?/THE STORY OF THE LONE RANGER™ (rev. ed. 1981), at 17.
2. Ibid., at 28.
3. Ibid., at 29.
4. Ibid., at 30.
5. Ibid., *passim.*
6. Ibid., at 83.
7. Ibid.
8. Ibid., at 25.
9. Ibid., at 86–88.
10. Ibid., at 123.
11. Ibid.
12. Ibid., *passim.*
13. Ibid., at 137, 139.
14. Ibid., at 141.
15. Ibid., at 201.
16. Ibid., at 197–200.
17. Ibid., at 235.
18. Ibid., at 178, 191.
19. Ibid., at 191.
20. Ibid., at 141.
21. Ibid., at 141, 145, 160.
22. Ibid., at 266.
23. Jones v. Republic Productions, 46 U.S.P.Q. 175 (9th Cir. 1940).
24. Lone Ranger v. Cox, 50 U.S.P.Q. 577 (W.D. S.C. 1941).
25. Lone Ranger v. Cox, 52 U.S.P.Q. 146 (4th Cir. 1942).

26. Lone Ranger v. Currey, 78 U.S.P.Q. 244 (M.D. Pa. 1948).
27. 78 U.S.P.Q. at 248.
28. ROTHEL, *supra* note 1, at 246–250.
29. Ibid., at 242, 247.
30. Ibid., at 248.
31. Ibid.
32. Ibid., at 250.
33. ANONYMOUS, SUPERMAN/FROM THE THIRTIES TO THE SEVENTIES (1971); GROSSMAN, SUPERMAN/SERIAL TO CEREAL (1976).
34. ANONYMOUS, *supra* note 33, at 7–8.
35. GROSSMAN, *supra* note 33.
36. ANONYMOUS, *supra* note 33, at 10.
37. Ibid.
38. GROSSMAN, *supra* note 33.
39. ANONYMOUS, *supra* note 33, at 11.
40. D. PETROU, THE MAKING OF SUPERMAN, THE MOVIE (1978).
41. Ibid., at 15.
42. Ibid. and ANONYMOUS, *supra* note 33.
43. ANONYMOUS, *supra* note 33, at 10–12.
44. Ibid., at 51, 333.
45. PETROU, *supra* note 40, at 17.
46. Ibid., at 26–27.
47. Ibid., at 11. Lest Dent is a pen name of Kenneth Robeson.
48. Siegel v. National Periodical Publications, 508 F.2d 909 (2d Cir. 1974).
49. 508 F.2d at 911–913.
50. Detective Comics v. Bruns Publications, 111 F.2d 432 (2d Cir. 1940).
51. 111 F.2d at 433. To the extent the Second Circuit is considering character per se rather than copyright in the larger sense, note that character and work appear to be inseparable. *See* chapters 5 and 9 for further discussion of relationships between characters and a work as a whole.
52. 111 F.2d at 433.
53. Ibid.
54. 111 F.2d at 434.
55. Detective Comics v. Fawcett Publications, 64 U.S.P.Q. 594 (S.D. N.Y. 1944).
56. National Comics Publications v. Fawcett Publications, 191 F.2d 594 (2d Cir. 1951).
57. 191 F.2d at 603. (Compare this language with that in the *Anti-Monopoly* cases reported in chapter 4.)

58. National Comics Publications v. Sive, 115 U.S.P.Q. 393 (Dec. Comm'r Pat. 1957).
59. DC Comics v. Powers, 201 U.S.P.Q. 99 (S.D. N.Y. 1978).
60. 201 U.S.P.Q. at 101.
61. Ibid.
62. Ibid.
63. 201 U.S.P.Q. at 102.
Character protection in merchandising is addressed in chapter 8.
64. Ibid.
65. Warner Bros. v. American Broadcasting Companies, 654 F.2d 204 (2d Cir. 1981).
66. 654 F.2d at 207.
67. Warner Bros. v. American Broadcasting Cos., 215 U.S.P.Q. 690. (2d Cir. 1982).
68. 215 U.S.P.Q. at 691.
69. 215 U.S.P.Q. at 692.
70. 215 U.S.P.Q. at 694. Note that the observation is not mere dictum. The issue of similarity between the characters could not arise in the absence of copyright in Superman himself—at least under New York law.
71. 215 U.S.P.Q. at 695.
72. 215 U.S.P.Q. at 696. (Asterisks and brackets in original.)
73. Columbia Broadcasting System, v. DeCosta, 377 F.2d 315 (1st Cir. 1967); *cert. den.* 389 U.S. 1007 (1968); DeCosta v. Columbia Broadcasting System, 520 F.2d 499 (1st Cir. 1975).
74. 377 F.2d at 315.
75. 377 F.2d at 320.
76. Columbia Broadcasting System v. DeCosta, 165 U.S.P.Q. 95 (Pat. Off. Trademark Trial and Appeal Bd. 1970).
77. CHICAGO TRIB., April 18, 1974, in Section 2.
78. 520 F.2d at 499.
79. 520 F.2d at 510.
80. 520 F.2d at 515.
81. THINGS TO COME January 1989 (Monthly catalog of Science Fiction Book Club).
82. S. WHITFIELD AND G. RODDENBERRY, THE MAKING OF STAR TREK (1968).
83. Ibid., Prologue (unpaginated).
84. Ibid., at 35, 169.
85. Ibid., at 393.
86. J. LICHTENBERG, S. MARSHAK AND J. WINSTON, STAR TREK LIVES! (1975).

87. Ibid., at 35.
88. Ibid., at 221–274.
89. *See, e.g.,* STAR TREK: THE NEW VOYAGES (MARSHAK and CULBREATH, eds. 1976); THE BEST OF TREK (IRWIN and LOVE, eds. 1978), and S. MARSHAK and M. CULBREATH, THE PRICE OF THE PHOENIX and THE FATE OF THE PHOENIX (1977 and 1979).
90. WHITFIELD, *supra* note 82, at 382–383, 393, 396–398.
91. LICHTENBERG, *supra* note 86, at 122.
92. Paramount Pictures Corp. v. Rubinowitz, 217 U.S.P.Q. 48 (E.D. N.Y. 1981).
93. *See* LICHTENBERG, *supra* note 86.
94. WHITFIELD, *supra* note 82, at 382 *ff.*
95. Ibid., at 233.
96. Ibid., at 125.
97. Ibid.
98. Ibid.

7

Case in Point: Tarzan of the Apes

INTELLECTUAL ORIGINS; COPYRIGHTABILITY

Feral Man and Noble Savages: The Traditions

Historical. Feral man and noble savages have been topics of fascination for as long as the human race has attributed to itself the characteristic of civilization.[1] Noble savage is the newer of the concepts, which tend to overlap. Feral individuals, especially wild children, have been reported with surprising frequency and are of intense interest to psychology and anthropology for what they can tell us of ourselves as individuals and as a social animal.

The concept of feral is a specific one. Historically (and legally), three kinds of animals have generally been recognized: wild, domestic, and feral. There is little difficulty in recognition of domesticated animals, but the distinction between wild and feral can become blurred. The significant difference lies in the basic nature of the species to which the individual belongs. No member of a wild species can be feral, although individuals can be domesticated. In contrast, only individuals of a domestic species can revert to the wild and thus become feral.

Feral nature, then, constitutes a return to the wild from domestication. That return is almost certainly the basis of our fascination with feral man. No matter how close to the conscious surface it may be allowed to rise, the subconscious longing to be a part of the wild world runs deep in the civilized mind.

True feral individuals are extremely rare in the real world. A very few individuals, usually children, have been reported to have been isolated from their civilized fellows, often to be nurtured by a domestic or wild species. These are the human equivalent of feral animals. In reality, it would appear there is none who would ever have been mistaken for a noble savage, best known to us in fiction, principally through Amerindians and Polynesians and the various persona portrayed by actor Jon Hall in such films as *The Hurricane* and *South of Pago Pago.*

Edgar Rice Burroughs's extraordinary creation, Tarzan of the Apes, is a feral man who is also portrayed as the noble savage. Whatever form he may take in one's imagination, Tarzan has in recent time assumed the archetypal image for feral humans.[2]

Scientific observations suggest that real feral individuals do not compare well at all with their counterparts in fantasy. But at the same time, they reveal some interesting parallels.[3] The reader of Burroughs's works in particular might well wonder how he came so close in so many ways. Did Burroughs have access to scholarly works from which he selected those characteristics that serve to render his Tarzan so enduring a hero? Were Tarzan a lightly fictionalized historical figure, his story could arguably lie outside the ambit of copyright protection.

But, unfortunately for the romanticists, science has discovered that too long an isolation from humanity or too strong an animal conditioning will permanently inhibit human development, and, in the latter instance, traces of the animal conditioning are never completely lost.[4] Very few feral individuals learn to like human society, several reportedly persisting in a longing for the wild. Clearly, any need for companionship takes the form of love for animals. There is a preference for the foster species or one closely related.[5]

Very few authentic feral individuals have been described as

adults. Victor, the "Wild Boy of Aveyron," stands out as perhaps the most satisfactory source of the character traits attributed to the modern fictional counterpart of the phenomenon.[6] With so few individuals adequately described, there is no way open for the exploration of this unfortunate but undeniably intriguing human condition. It is necessary, then, to turn to literary sources to search out some basis of the universal fascination with Tarzan and lesser noble savages.

Literature. The literary wild man of Western civilization goes back to the historian Herodotus and to classical mythology. But he is to be found throughout the world. Persia had its "bear-teachers" and Japan its "nursing monkeys."[7] He is found in the Old Testament in the great rebels against the Lord: the God-challengers. These rebels are comparable to the heroes of Greek literature.[8]

If one wishes to seek out Tarzan's remote literary ancestors, there are plenty to be found. Even Shakespeare can be cited as one of many sources for antecedents—in Caliban.[9] Over time the wild man as noble savage has been shown in the arts as an Amerindian, African, and South Sea Islander, among any number of others. The characterization, however, remains much the same: "brave, loyal, stoic, aloof, and inclined to be sententious in his comparisons between native cultures and imported European civilizations." The character "is determined not by science but by changing cultural attitudes toward the natural and the primitive which he represents."[10]

Certain aspects of the wild man as noble savage can be found in works as diverse as *Robinson Crusoe, Swiss Family Robinson,* and *Frankenstein.* The noble savage aspect is also found in *Atala & Rene,* originally written in 1801 and 1802, respectively.[11]

The idea continues to evolve with the passage of time and consequent changes in the collective intellect. The wild man, and one of his most popular representatives, Tarzan of the Apes, is, then, a part of our basic nature—whatever its source may be—according to scholars of anthropology and psychology. Hence, the fascinating use of this type in the arts. Tarzan, then, while a unique literary property, is one of several heroes of this particular type.

Most critics would trace Tarzan's immediate lineage to

Mowgli, a character in *The Jungle Books*.[12] Close reading of the two bodies of work, however, strongly suggests that there is far more to Tarzan of the Apes at every conceivable level than literary critics have been willing to concede.

The Jungle Books, including the stories of Mowgli, were written in the years 1894 and 1895. There is some suggestion they were influenced by *Uncle Remus*.[13] Unlike Burroughs's novels, at least one tale of Mowgli, "Mowgli's Brothers," is told from the point of view of the wolves, Mowgli's adoptive family. These and all the other creatures of the jungle speak among themselves in ordinary English. In fact, the stories are very British in attitude and are quite obviously intended more for children than for adults. All the creatures instinctively recognize a special destiny for Mowgli as man's cub.[14]

In keeping with the intended audience, there is a gentle humor tracing its way through the tales of Mowgli: he encountered wolves of every size and color—"from badger-coloured veterans who could handle a buck alone, to young black three-year-olds, who thought they could."[15] Kipling never takes Mowgli into manhood: "So Mowgli went away and hunted . . . in the jungle from that day on. But he was not always alone, because, years afterward, he became a man and married.

"But that is a story for grown-ups."[16]

Burroughs's character study of Tarzan, the adult feral individual, once gleaned from his genre adventures, hardly represents any decline in imaginative quality. The intelligent child is enthralled with Mowgli and wonders what will become of him. Through Burroughs, the adult can find out what might have become of him. But to do so the adult must pursue the character through the thickets and quagmires of the plot devices and less-than-subtle humor of the genre in which Burroughs wrote with such notable success. For some it is a delight; for others tedium.

Context for intellectual property in Tarzan. Burroughs's Tarzan springs from a number of roots but is unique and uniquely protected through both copyright and trademark, as well as unfair competition theory, as will be described in detail in the remainder of this chapter.

In the context of source for purposes of copyright law, and

especially with regard to characters as scènes à faire, it is worth noting that the twenty-two characteristics of the archetypal hero can be ascribed to Tarzan of the Apes.[17] Under the judicial "pattern" approach, were "the hero" copyrighted, Tarzan would be an infringement. More significantly, any feral heroes subsequent to Tarzan and paralleling his nature and circumstances will present some judicial quandries. Direct plagiarism might be the only actionable copyright infringement in terms of the first few novels (at least the first of which has now lapsed into the public domain by passage of time). In fact, the proprietors of Tarzan seem to have tacitly acknowledged the situation through the cases they have brought and, most particularly, the nature of reported settlements.[18]

The Creation of Tarzan

Edgar Rice Burroughs, author and proprietor. This is hardly the proper setting for a lengthy profile detailing either the life of Edgar Rice Burroughs or his writings at large. To date, both have been thoroughly explored in five books by four different authors.[19] The first book, a biography, was published in 1965, the last, a critique of his major works of fiction, in 1986. In addition, a recent and wide-ranging compendium of "proper names, words, phrases and concepts" from the Burroughs canon includes entries drawn from the Ape as imagined by Burroughs to references from classical Greek literature and beyond.[20]

Burroughs, while successful and popular, had frequently to call upon his sense of humor to salvage a variety of situations the author found disturbing. For example, in a 1929 letter to his brother, Burroughs urged the older man to write but to avoid fiction unless it came easily. The market was then seeking nonfiction at historical levels.[21] In giving advice to young writers, he elaborated his personal philosophy of fiction, advising his correspondent to take neither himself nor his work too seriously inasmuch as fiction is absolutely unessential, except as entertainment. Burroughs said that the reader has a right to expect entertainment and relaxation, not instruction. The reader certainly does not want to think.[22]

Tarzan is surely the medium through which Burroughs, the

man, is made known to most people. Fans who know only the two myths (Tarzan's and the one woven about Burroughs's innumerable "failures") are missing something. Burroughs was a successful man who sought out adventure on a grand scale, and he was a man with a tremendous sense of fun, humor, and the ridiculous. He was also an astute businessman, notwithstanding some notable lapses. Tarzan and the promotion of Tarzan bridge the gap between the man and the businessman. Tarzan is among the first of what might be called "cartoon heroes."[23]

Development and marketing of the character. The ape-man's beginnings in pulp fiction are comparable to the Lone Ranger's in radio, Superman's in comics, and Mr. Spock's in television. Each character stands representative of the most popular of the popular media of his time. Each has engendered phenomenal success, which has transcended that in his particular medium of origin. Each has launched an equally phenomenal marketing blitz, which has remained active through at least two generations of fans. In Tarzan's case, one man is almost single-handedly responsible for the failures as well as the successes.

With Tarzan the passage of generations was first reflected in series dust jackets and illustrations. Something of each generation is suggested through its peculiar version of the apeman. But Burroughs never bound Tarzan to the printed page.

There was an early British stage production of the first novel with bits from the second. While it played the provinces, it never made London and failed in New York with critics and audiences alike. It was asserted that the impossible had been attempted. If a play was impossible, it is even harder to believe a condensation for the vaudeville circuit. Here Burroughs' sense of humor held sway; he encouraged "real, honest-to-God Burlesque."[24]

Licensing, along with the marketing of secondary products, has been a major component of the Tarzan cycle, but dramatizations have always been the most interesting—if not the most important—vehicle for the character. They have assumed an almost completely independent force in presentation and even development of the persona known as Tarzan of the Apes.

Tarzan was an expression of Burroughs's need for fantastic escape from the mundane. Tarzan was also a veritable gold mine.[25]

Illustrative of Burroughs's involvement in the marketing of Tarzan is the evolution of the radio program. In 1930 it was suggested that Burroughs read from one of his novels on a national hookup for fifteen minutes each evening. Burroughs would receive sixty percent of the proceeds. In 1931 the event had not yet come to pass, possibly because Burroughs had become cautious in his intermedia marketing efforts. He "believed the new field of radio could provide great money-making opportunities and he was determined to find a reliable and imaginative organization to handle the marketing of *Tarzan.* Above all, [Burroughs] was waiting for presentation ideas that would do justice to the ape-man."[26]

The show went on in 1932, running fifteen minutes, six days a week. Burroughs maintained a close scrutiny of the scripts. While he, himself, enjoyed a hearty laugh, he firmly disapproved of laughter and comedy when written for Tarzan. Burroughs kept a close watch on the characterization.[27]

When the three-year contract and option for renewal was entered for the radio rights, Burroughs kept an eagle eye on just where most of the profits would be going, and he was already pondering how his own corporation could secure control. Forty stations ran the show with nearly $1 million per year charged to sponsors. The fact that Burroughs had launched his own publishing enterprise in 1931, despite the depression, suggests his daring, and possibly reckless, sense of business.[28]

Delineation of Tarzan

While Tarzan of the Apes needs no introduction to those who know him through the writings of Edgar Rice Burroughs, the sophistication of his character will come as a surprise to anyone who only knows the portrayal by Johnny Weissmuller. Tarzan of the Apes is noble savage, wild man, and hero in one lithe, bronzed package, which has for a half century intrigued audiences of all ages and of multiple cultures.[29]

A reading of Burroughs's *Tarzan of the Apes*, *Return of Tarzan*, *Jungle Tales of Tarzan*, *Son of Tarzan*, and either *Tarzan and the Jewels of Opar* or *Tarzan the Untamed* is sufficient to reveal Tarzan as the archetypal hero. This perception of Tarzan is reflected in an article written at the height of the resurgence of interest in Burroughs's writings, which emerged more than a decade after the author's death.[30] The article was devoted to the perceived correlation between the heroic epic and science fiction, especially that of Burroughs with specific reference to the author's series set on Mars.

Tarzan spends his first twenty years in the jungle. He has succeeded in teaching himself to read and print in English (possibly because the Grey Apes are capable of something very close to language) and eventually rises to leadership among the apes. He is in his late teens before he encounters Caucasians. Tarzan is returned to civilization by the Frenchman, Paul d'Arnot, and eventually marries an American, Jane Porter.

Described as more Apollo than Hercules, Tarzan often seems very like the heroic Amerindian of popular culture. Handsome in the best classical sense, the ape-man's face reflects the best of both sides of his unique character. His eyes, in particular, reflect strength of character.

What renders Burroughs's Tarzan at once unique and fascinating is the combination of character and abilities derived from two utterly different environments. While Tarzan's physical attributes are completely dependable, he appears to have little control over which aspect of his self will come to the fore—ape or man.

Tarzan is, after all, feral man, with all the strangeness and the deep ambivalence inherent to that concept. He has the dignity both of the beast and of the heritage behind noble blood. Dignity requires intelligence. Once again, Tarzan is amply endowed. From the beginning, Tarzan's very survival is attributable to his quick mind. But, somewhere along the line, in ways left unreported by Burroughs, Tarzan manages rather a wide-ranging education. Numerous examples of his articulate knowledge of the arcane can be found scattered through the novels. Burroughs's ape-man is something of a displaced Renaissance Man.

Nobility and honor are inherent to Tarzan of the Apes, notwithstanding his bestiality. Tarzan is never at a loss as to what his own nobility demands, for all its naiveté. And yet he is never allowed to seem either pompous or foolish. Fortunately, Tarzan's anger, with or without the savage touch, is sparingly aroused and serves the man well.

Ever ambivalent in the face of his humanity (unlike Mowgli, who is smug in his), Tarzan moves from one extreme to the other in his reaction to his own species. Tarzan's initial disaffection never leaves him, but it is not so much individual as collective humanity that he abhors. The ape-man remains suspicious of the species but finds both enemies and friends among its individuals.

As important as are Tarzan's characteristic reactions to his fellows, their responses to him in many ways reveal more of his character. Tarzan arouses justifiable fear in enemies, but among other people he is recognized as a leader. Tarzan possesses strength, majesty, and ferocity. While men are inspired (or intimidated) by Tarzan's courage and inherent capacity for leadership, women inevitably fall in love with him.

Those familiar with the stolid heroes of the genre in which Burroughs wrote will not be surprised at the cluster of feminine hearts held prisoner— in all innocence—by the Lord of the Jungle. What sets Burroughs's character apart from all the rest is some of the detail that might easily be overlooked in the compelling rush of the adventures. There is a unique subtlety to the character reflected in the diverse women who fall for the ape-man. Unlike most heroes of his genre, Tarzan is amply endowed with a libido.

An absolute need for freedom on all levels is the driving force behind Tarzan's every move. Yet that need is tempered by his steadfast love for Jane; a love that prevails over all despite the temptations offered by other women. Tarzan is also steadfast in his friendships, often at the expense of freedom. Of all the ape-man's noble qualities, perhaps the most noble is his profound sense of loyalty. He is utterly fearless, but without stupidity or arrogance. Finally, and this trait is the unshakeable companion of the ambivalence, Tarzan is perpetually lonely. He is not simply alone.

The foregoing description is but a small sampling of Burroughs's master touch in character development. Whenever he writes of Tarzan, this author is profoundly evocative. Were the character of Tarzan not a personification of the intriguing wild man/noble savage, still Burroughs would have the power to captivate the reader.

While countless children of all ages may have thrilled to the adventures of Tarzan in the original novels, the tales are intended for an adult audience. In fact, Burroughs demonstrates a surprising degree of sophistication. His observations simultaneously comparing and contrasting animal behavior to human behavior are pointedly witty and provide substantial food for adult thought.

LEGAL MANAGEMENT; COPYRIGHT, TRADEMARK, AND LICENSING

The Literary Properties

Burroughs began his phenomenal career as a writer of fiction in 1912, at the age of 37. His first work, a story entitled "Under the Moons of Mars," published in *All-Story* magazine, set the pattern for things to come. The story became the book, *A Princess of Mars*, and literary history was in the making. Sequels were not far behind. Neither was Tarzan of the Apes. Begun in December of 1911, the novel was completed in less than six months. The story was first published by *All-Story* in late 1912. The first McClurg edition of the book was published in 1914.[31]

From 1919 through 1920 almost two million copies of Burroughs's books were sold in the United States. In the last half of 1920, *Tarzan of the Apes* alone sold 55,000 copies. Burroughs's income in 1921 approached $100,000, a figure characterized in 1986 as "astonishing."[32] By 1921 the author was receiving additional royalties from foreign sales.[33]

By 1922 *Tarzan of the Apes* had been translated into seven languages and offers were pending for three more. This was the year in which Burroughs entered an agreement with Munsey to guarantee the publisher the first reading of the author's entire fictional output.[34] By 1924 Burroughs's heavy foreign sales notably included many sales to Russians. In fact, the total Russian printing of 250,000 proved to be insufficient. Tarzan was extremely popular in that country despite disdain from certain quarters. The resolution to Russian demand was another sign of things to come: six Tarzan titles were pirated and sold as $.60 paperbacks.[35]

Burroughs consulted at length with accountants and attorneys before being advised to become a corporation. In 1922 incorporation by an artist was a unique concept. No author had ever taken the step. The California corporation was organized on March 26, 1923. In another month Burroughs had transferred to the corporation all the rights, title, and interest in his current and future literary efforts. The stock was distributed to the immediate family, with Burroughs taking the controlling interest.[36]

Burroughs's earliest encounters with matters of intellectual property from the legal perspective were accusations in 1926 that he had committed plagiarism. The credibility of the accusation loses something by reason of its context: it was levelled by the German press in the midst of uproar over *Tarzan the Untamed*, a story of anti-German sentiment. It was alleged that in 1911 a French writer published a piece about a family of three who were shipwrecked off Asia on their way to India. Although all three end up on an uninhabited island, the parents are killed by wild gorillas. The surviving child is raised by a female gorilla and returned to Paris years later. It seemed to matter little that Burroughs had never seen the work, had no knowledge of it, and read no French. In any event, the accusation was dismissed as mere fabrication. The alleged novel was never located.[37]

For the most part, Burroughs and, later, his corporation were on the complaining end of any lawsuit arising from plagiarism in all its variants and permutations. But this vigilance does not reflect a mean spirit. When in 1926 a teenager in Atlanta formed an Edgar Rice Burroughs club, the author not only replied to the teenager's letter but suggested that the membership write and present a short play based on one of his works.[38]

Despite such generosity, not to mention a plethora of licensing agreements, many people felt free to appropriate the name of Tarzan without resort to permission or payment. Some people simply assumed the name for professional or publicity purposes. Initially these usurpations were met with nothing more than resignation. The incidences were just too widespread to detect, much less restrain. Among these were: Tarzans appearing in vaudeville and for a New York film company, Tarzan wine, Tarzan chocolates, a Tarzan cafe in Berlin, a (successful) pacer by the name of Tarzan Grattan, and a registered dog. There was even Tarzan bond paper, and Burroughs used it.[39]

Contractual Protection of the Character

An attitude of tolerant humor and the belief that the multitude of unauthorized uses were helpful in spreading a mild and pleasant publicity could not last. In 1933 MGM, on the brink of its own marketing coup, prompted a cautionary note on infringement from Burroughs. In 1939 he sent a warning letter to a wrestler who was using Tarzan's name.[40] Since that time Burroughs and his successor, Edgar Rice Burroughs, Inc., have assiduously protected their intellectual properties, repelling all infringement with a vengeance.

Whenever Burroughs failed to protect his works, the immediate lesson was not soon forgotten. For example, having lost rights in several of his earliest works through ignorance, Burroughs thereafter persisted in selling only the first serial rights of the subsequent works. All other rights the author retained.[41]

All novelists can take an obvious lesson or two from Burroughs's many disappointments with the cinema. He single-handedly went far in revealing the profound gap that exists between any novel and its film adaptation. In Burroughs's own time the whole concept was innovative. Translation from the written word through the conventions of film, now taken for granted, was then just coming into its own. Burroughs was a pioneer here as elsewhere. But fans of Burroughs's ape-man can only empathize with the author in that the vehicle that has served to place Tarzan at the center of his creator's literary status is that notorious misrepresentation, film.[42]

In 1916, having previously sold an unrelated scenario to a film company (without notable result), Burroughs entered into an agreement for the production of *Tarzan of the Apes*. Burroughs's remuneration consisted of $5,000 cash, another $50,000 in stock and five percent of the gross receipts. The film finally premiered in January of 1918 in the absence of Burroughs, who was thoroughly exasperated with every aspect of the result.[43]

In 1920 the serial version of *The Son of Tarzan* was produced; Burroughs, himself, edited it for release as a feature. But the efforts at personal involvement in production persisted only until 1924 when Burroughs was struggling under the weight of financial and other difficulties. Burroughs's efforts to market Tarzan in the cinema were perpetually rocky. In 1922 Burroughs made a major lapse in his business judgment: he sold outright the film rights to *Jungle Tales of Tarzan* and *Tarzan and the Jewels of Opar*. The former became *Tarzan the Mighty*. Its only relationship to the book was in the shared name, Tarzan.[44]

The second film, *Tarzan the Tiger,* had little to bind it to the underlying novel. Burroughs was at a loss, since he had sold the story years before. Recognizing futility when he saw it, Burroughs did not squander his time on an effort to control production. Interestingly, this film was graced with a sound track, but efforts to secure payment for the sound rights failed. The lawyers involved could not attach a value to the new rights or even determine whether they possessed any value distinct from those included in the purchase of the story.[45]

In the midtwenties Burroughs received $5,000 in advance and the promise of ten percent of the net profits to prepare the theme for the production of *The Daughter of Tarzan*. Nothing came of the scheme, and Burroughs declined to accept this fee for a switch to *Tarzan and the Golden Lion*. At that point two producers were vying for film rights to that novel, but all manner of problems developed. In 1927 one producer finally completed the film only to be sued by the other. Somehow a contract was signed and release followed, but the film was unsuccessful.[46]

Tarzan the Fearless of 1929 represented nothing but a repetition of past mistakes. In the early thirties, an agreement was reached with MGM. But film rights were already subject to controversy when production commenced on *Tarzan the Ape-Man,* which apparently was never intended to be—and most certainly never was—*Tarzan of the Apes.* Even while *Tarzan the Fearless* was going forward with Buster Crabbe, negotiations were in progress with Sol Lesser and MGM. Lesser acquired the rights to the Buster Crabbe vehicle.[47]

No small part of Burroughs's business savvy was dedicated to the character of Tarzan. Long before the case of Sam Spade came before the courts, Burroughs was sorting through his intellectual property rights and using language that sounds very like trademark law. As Burroughs put it to one film studio, the name of Tarzan was worth more to his creator than any cinema rights in the stories. Furthermore, Burroughs was concerned about the studio's future releases. He was well aware that films wholly unrelated to Tarzan would be produced under that name "so that in a little while the word would be entirely meaningless to the motion picture public so far as my stories were concerned."[48]

Burroughs was to complain constantly of the major diversions from his characters and stories in the films. Characteristically, he was far from reticent on the subject. In a 1922 letter to his brother, the author asserted that no one in the film industry had any conception of either the story or the character, as he conceived of them: "Whatever beauty there was in the character of Tarzan or in the stories themselves, was not brought out," even though the films did well in box office receipts.[49]

As a mark of his own peculiar mix of marketing acumen, litigious spirit, and generosity, Burroughs permitted the California community developing on his former California ranch to assume its name: Tarzana.[50] The movie cowboy Ken Maynard was authorized by Burroughs to use the name Tarzan for his horse; there was even a Maynard film entitled, *Come on, Tarzan.*[51]

Because Burroughs was constantly embroiled in strong-willed negotiations and frequent legal battles in bringing Tarzan and his other characters to the public, it comes as something of a surprise that the earliest known unauthorized film was *The Adventures of the Chinese Tarzan* made in the 1940s. More surprising: if legal action followed, it is not recorded. On the other hand, Sol Lesser legally confiscated a 1943 pirated version (Turkish) of *Tarzan's Revenge.*[52]

THE CASES

The Preliminaries

One case did make it to adjudication during Burroughs's lifetime.[53] By the forties Tarzan was a registered trademark "appropriated" to a variety of merchandise. "Tar-Gin," for which an application had been submitted for a variety of clothing and accessories, was held by the Examiner of Trademarks to be "confusingly similar" and denied registration. This decision was affirmed by the Commissioner of Patents, even though Tar-Gin was a contraction of the applicant's name, Taragin.

The earliest reported litigation and resultant appeals associated with Tarzan of the Apes had nothing to do with Burroughs or his corporation.[54] The matter did, however, address copyright in the context of contract law. At issue was the film, *Tarzan's Magic Fountain,* which allegedly represented an infringement of Ilsa Lahn Weitzenkorn's screenplay *Tarzan in the Land of Eternal Youth,* submitted at the request of Sol Lesser and other defendants pursuant to an oral agreement. In consideration of the submission Weitzenkorn was to be paid reasonable value and receive customary screen credit. The ultimate film, although its action centered on a hidden land of eternal youth, represented rather a different series of events than those of the original composition.

In the trial court, all three of the plaintiff's counts were dismissed on demurrers. The trial court had read her composition and viewed Lesser's film, as did the California Supreme Court. The plaintiff, of course, argued that her complaint presented issues of fact deserving to be heard. Notably among these were the basic copyright issues of originality, similarity, access, and copying.

Among the questions resolved in this matter, based in part on the California code, is whether infringement can support a case in breach of contract (in addition to the more common tort actions). The holding was that some of the statutory copyright rights are entirely contractual and thus the contractual matter was properly addressed. Thereupon the copyright issues were to be addressed. The starting point of these issues was the originality of the plaintiff's composition. If it is without originality, there is no protectible property in it and, therefore, no question of fact to be determined by a jury.

There was contention as to the extent to which the court should take judicial notice of the body of published literature in considering originality. In the end the high court took judicial notice of the fact that in the realm of fiction certain popular characters called Tarzan, Jane, and Cheta live in Africa and that the myth of a fountain of eternal youth is one of the oldest known to man.[55]

Anything beyond that would be subject to proof. Hence, were originality of concept the sole criterion, the case should not have been dismissed. Instead the case depended on originality of expression in form and manner, of characterization development, and of sequence of events. Given some degree of originality, consideration of similarity between Weitzenkorn's work and the film was in order. But essential differences were clear from a superficial comparison of the two works.[56]

Still, with regard to the contract before the court, the California Supreme Court conceded that, even though improbable, Weitzenkorn might be able to show an express contract whereby Lesser had agreed to pay for her material notwithstanding its legal protectability or some minimal use of it. To this extent, two of the plaintiff's counts were held to be improperly dismissed, and the court remanded for the defendants' answer to them.[57]

There was an interesting dissent based specifically in the change in statutory language that gave rise to the action. Prior to the change, an idea might be subject to protection under California law. The amendment, however, limited recognition to an exclusive ownership in its representation or expression alone.

The dissenting justice expressed the fear, which must be particularly relevant in Hollywood, that

> by minor changes in the sequence of events and the characterizations, the plagiarist may escape liability under this holding. . . . This unnecessarily harsh result will not have the effect of promoting the progress of literature. Authors, anxious to find a market for their work are not in an advantageous bargaining position to insist that the one to whom the composition is submitted sign a contract agreeing to compensate them if the work is used. . . . The movie industry is constantly looking for "ideas" and "plots" which it develops as it sees fit. . . . To extend protection only to the expression and representation is to give no protection at all.[58]

That this issue remains viable is manifested in the contract action Art Buchwald has brought in the context of Eddie Murphy's film *Coming to America*. The two cases appear to be identical.[59]

The California court seemingly affords Burroughs and the authors of the Tarzan films short shrift in asserting that the characters Tarzan, Jane, and Cheta are well known, old, and *in the public domain* along with the fountain of youth. They are indeed well known. Of that there can be no doubt. But whether they are in the public domain is quite another question. Certainly, a comparison with the fountain of youth in the context of intellectual property is a gross overstatement and ill considered. This court seemingly used a term of legal art in the sense a layman would.

Direct Plagiarism

A surprising case arose in the midsixties—the height of the republication of the Tarzan novels and other works by Burroughs.[60] The case is surprising for two reasons; it involves blatant plagiarism, and the author's pseudonym was actually taken from the name of the villain of the directly plagiarized work. It is as though the gauntlet had been flung at the feet of Tarzan's proprietors.

The reported opinion is scant, consisting of nothing more than three paragraphs, the denial of the motion, and reference to the order. But the second paragraph is illuminating in this context: One of Burroughs's counts charges that defendants' publications were "calculated to and did represent, suggest and imply falsely and fraudulently (a) that the character and characterization of 'Tarzan' and the stories in which said character appeared were, or included, the literary efforts of Edgar Rice Burroughs or (b) plaintiffs' association, sponsorship or connection with defendants'... publications..." thereby "deceiving, misleading and confusing the public."[61] This action in unfair competition, at least for purposes of the motion before the court, is based more in trademark than in copyright.

Copyrights and Contracts

The MGM contract. In 1931 Burroughs entered into a written contract with Hollywood's legendary MGM. In retrospect, at least from the perspective of protecting the literary Tarzan specifically, that contract was among Burroughs's major lapses in business judgment.

For the lump sum of $20,000 and the payment of $1,000 a week for a five-week stint as advisor and consultant, Burroughs gave MGM "'the right to create and write an original story, using as one of the characters therein, the character of 'Tarzan,' which character was originally created by the author."[62]

Surprisingly, there was no provision for continuing royalties, especially given the remainder of the pertinent contractual provisions.[63] Additional characters from the Tarzan books then existing could be included. The title of the film, to be selected by MGM, was to include more than one word, excluding titles listed in an exhibit attached to the agreement.

Not surprisingly, paragraph 14 of the contract granted MGM the right to make a photoplay from that original story. But, what may come as an additional surprise are the further rights to reissue, to remake, and to produce additional photoplays from MGM's original. The only limitations on those further rights were the requirement of substantial basis in the MGM original and the prohibition of any material change or material departure from it.[64]

The MGM cases. MGM did create an original story and did make the film *Tarzan the Ape-Man* from the story. Few people around the world remain ignorant of Johnny Weissmuller's Tarzan and Maureen O'Sullivan's Jane. But in 1959 there was a remake which has been seen by few. It may have been a poor example of cinema artistry, but, according to the California court, it represented no breach of that 1931 agreement.[65] At issue after a viewing of the 1932 and 1959 versions of the film was whether the plaintiff, Edgar Rice Burroughs, Inc. (ERB) had stated sufficient facts to constitute a cause of action.[66] Here, the plaintiff's cause actually depended upon an *absence* of substantial similarity.

In addressing this crucial matter, the court held inherent to the express rights held by MGM the implied right to update and modernize clothes, customs, dialogue, mood, and tempo; to use current modern techniques of color and camera; and to adapt the story to the way people live and look at life in this and future generations, rather than in the generation in which the original photoplay was made.[67]

In entering summary judgment for the defendants, the court found, as a matter of law, the contract to be unambiguous and thus not open to interpretation. The two films were found to be based on substantially the same story without material change or material departure. ERB appealed.[68] But appeal was unavailing; judgment for MGM was affirmed. The appellate court did note that the crucial issue of similarity is substantially the same as that determinative in plagiarism and infringement actions. With reference to a comparable precedent in which the corresponding contractual arrangement prohibited revisions not approved by the author, the California court noted that it had been held "that as long as appropriate expression of the theme, thought and main action of the original story is retained 'scenery, action, and characters may be added . . . and even supplant subordinate portions.' "[69]

Tarzan was not back in court until 1980.[70] MGM had embarked on yet another remake, this time featuring the talents of John and Bo Derek. However, there was an added complication.

In 1976 the federal copyright statute had been amended. Section 304(c), as amended, allowed for the termination by the original author or representatives of that author of grants or licenses under an extant copyright. The grant or license had to have been executed before January 1, 1978, the effective date of the statute's major amendments. Termination had to be effected within a five-year interval specified in the provision itself, on a two-year advance written notice to all grantees. Derivative works arising from a grant subject to actual termination could be continued only if they were in progress prior to actual termination. The grant itself would remain in effect until termination went into effect.

The Burroughs family thought they had found the solution to the problem MGM had been posing all through the years. They terminated all grants Edgar Rice Burroughs had effected to ERB. But they made two major errors. They acted in advance of the effective date of the statute and failed to notify MGM of the termination. Moreover, the constraints of the statutory timing could not have prevented the Derek production of *Tarzan the Ape-Man*.

In any event, as the Southern District of New York noted, the books and the films each proceeded under their own independent copyrights, and the Burroughs family, in their haste, had even omitted from the notice certain Tarzan titles, leaving those titles available for MGM's selection of characters. Whatever the validity of this reasoning, had notice been properly served in the first instance, it can come as no surprise that the ERB's motion for preliminary injunction to halt production was denied. In short, the termination effort was a legal nullity and could have no legal effect on MGM's rights pursuant to that 1931 contract.

An interesting aside to this abortive attempt to put a halt to MGM's legal hold on its vision of the Tarzan character was the concern that certain negotiations with Warner Bros. would be placed in jeopardy if another film went forward. Warner had tentatively entitled its planned film *Greystoke*.

Undaunted, the Burroughs family was back before the New York district in the summer of 1981.[71] This time both sides had filed motions for summary judgment. Termination of rights under copyright remained at issue. The Dereks' film was ready for release and distribution.

The plaintiffs were particularly disturbed by the film's R rating. Bo Derek appeared in the nude in a particularly unsavory scene. The court, showing questionable sensitivity, found nothing offensive. Even worse, however, was the nasty scene underlying the end credits, when an orangutan all but violates a giggling Jane while Tarzan indolently observes. Here the film incarnation of the ape-man is completely out of character.

The first substantive question before the court was whether the 1931 grant to MGM was of copyright property. The district court answered in the affirmative with some highly pertinent language: "It cannot be said that [copyright in a literary work such as TARZAN OF THE APES] contemplates protection of only the plot, leaving the characters free for public exploitation for, as in the case of plays, the "characters and sequence of incident [are] the substance."[72] But it is only well-developed characters who are subject to protection, characters such as those in Burroughs's Tarzan books. They are protected by the copyright in the work itself. If the character in question is granted in part to another, that grant arises from copyright, as is the case here.

Thereupon, the court inflicted upon itself a viewing of all three MGM efforts—1932, 1959, 1981—looking for substantial similarities and for material changes or departures. Somehow it found the similarities material but not the changes or departures.

All motions were granted, the result being that the attempted termination was held ineffective—again. The film was released. On appeal, the decision was affirmed.[73] Having decided that the termination was defective, the Second Circuit made no effort to address the matter of copyright in characters in reaching its decision. It does, however, speak to this matter in a note.[74] There the court observes that whether Tarzan himself is copyrightable might have been in issue should MGM have embarked on yet another remake before 1987 (when the novel *Tarzan of the Apes* entered the public domain).

In yet another note the court observes that

> [t]here is no occasion in this litigation to consider the intriguing question whether a grant of rights to a book in which a well-delineated character first appears constitutes a relinquishment by the author of his own "sequel" rights to reuse this original character, or whether, at least as between ... creator ... and the creator's grantee, an author retains his own sequel rights, in addition to [those] conveyed to his grantee, at least in the absence of an explicit relinquishment of such personal rights.[75]

Once again some of the language scattered throughout the reasoning is extremely interesting. Initially, the appellate court observed that the 1981 film is not substantially similar to *Tarzan of the Apes* (with limited exceptions as permitted by the 1931 agreement). An interesting state of legal affairs is expressed: legally, there are in fact (at least) *two* Tarzans.

One Tarzan recognized by the courts is the Tarzan created, nurtured, and fiercely championed by Edgar Rice Burroughs. The other Tarzan, often denigrated by Burroughs throughout his own lifetime, sprang from Burroughs's creation through a contractual lineage. This Tarzan was more immediately created by the cinema. True, the source of both Tarzans is ultimately Edgar Rice Burroughs, but they represent two very different images, as has already been discussed here and in a plethora of other writings both published and private. As the court put it, "the few purported similarities either are so general as to be meaningless, or are not similarities at all."[76]

Tarzan, the Trademark

In addition to Tarzan's courtroom appearances arising from mainstream films, he was also an issue in the Central District of California in his trademark capacity.[77] An X-rated film entitled *Tarz & Jane & Boy & Cheeta* had been produced. Setting out lists of itemized findings of fact and of conclusions of law, the district court specified six Certificates of Registration of the "mark" Tarzan. One of these certificates is for books, comic books, and newspaper cartoons. The others are for a variety of merchandise. The mark is also registered in thirty-odd foreign countries. Copyrights in publications employing Tarzan and Jane are recognized as well, as are the forty authorized films.

With reference to the attempted X-rated entry into the Tarzan film legacy the court found that members of the public at large recognize Tarzan, individually, and with Jane and the others in relationship to entertainment goods and services exclusively supplied or authorized by the plaintiff. The court then found dilution in ERB's lack of control over the X-rated film. It also found the likelihood of confusion as to origin and of passing off by the defendants. Finally, the court found that Burroughs's goodwill would be impaired.

On those findings of fact, the court held that a temporary restraining order and preliminary injunction are appropriate where infringement of a registered trademark and a registered copyright claim exist—and to restrain acts of unfair competition, such as those perpetrated by these defendants. A disclaimer by the infringing party is insufficient protection. Two specific conclusions are crucial to Tarzan's legal and hence literary future:

1. Famous character names in copyrighted works may not be used by others during the life of the copyright without the authorization of the copyright proprietor.
2. The trademark Tarzan is a strong mark that is entitled to protection against the likelihood of confusion as to the source or origin of goods and/or services or dilution of its value.[78]

Given the status of copyright protection of characters in the Ninth Circuit, the source of the first proposition is something of a mystery. In any event, the two propositions neatly conclude the foregoing materials as a demonstration of the mechanics behind long-term protection of a character so popular as to be forever teetering at the precipice over the public domain.

Burroughs and his successors have utilized the full complement of legal tools in retaining the intellectual properties represented in Tarzan. Their unique mixture of success, failure, and outright lapse in policing these properties has led to a peculiar divergence in the delineation of the character itself. Artistically, two Tarzans actually reign in the minds of the consuming public. Perhaps it does not matter, especially since both trace their lineage to Edgar Rice Burroughs as the ultimate source. Moreover, the epitome of the contemporary hero of the popular arts, Tarzan of the Apes exists in multiple delineations in the individual imaginations of each reader or viewer.

NOTES

1. *See, e.g.*, Zingg, *Feral Man and Extreme Cases of Isolation,* 53 AM. J. PSYCH. 487 (1940); L. MALSON, WOLF CHILDREN AND THE PROBLEM OF HUMAN NATURE (1972); C. MACLEAN, THE WOLF CHILDREN (1977), and THE WILD MAN WITHIN (DUDLEY AND NOVAK, eds. 1972).

2. Burroughs's novels of Tarzan have been in print since they were first published. They are available in a number of editions, including those specified below. For further information contact George T. McWhorter, Curator of the Edgar Rice Burroughs Collection at the University of Louisville's Ekstrom Library. TARZAN OF THE APES (Grosset & Dunlap, 1914); THE RETURN OF TARZAN (McClurg, 1915); THE BEASTS OF TARZAN (Grosset & Dunlap, 1916); THE SON OF TARZAN (Burt, 1918); TARZAN AND THE JEWELS OF OPAR (Grosset & Dunlap, 1918); JUNGLE TALES OF TARZAN (McClurg, 1919); TARZAN THE UNTAMED (Grosset & Dunlap, 1920); TARZAN THE TERRIBLE (Grosset & Dunlap, 1921); TARZAN AND THE GOLDEN LION (Grosset & Dunlap, 1923); TARZAN AND THE ANT-MEN (Grosset & Dunlap, 1924); TARZAN, LORD OF THE JUNGLE (Grosset & Dunlap, 1928); TARZAN AND THE LOST EMPIRE (Metropolitan, 1928–1929); TARZAN AT THE EARTH'S CORE (Grosset & Dunlap, 1930); TARZAN THE INVINCIBLE (Grosset & Dunlap, 1930–1931); TARZAN TRIUMPHANT (Grosset & Dunlap, 1931–1932); TARZAN AND THE LION-MAN (Grosset & Dunlap, 1934); TARZAN AND THE LEOPARD-MEN (ERB, Inc., 1935); TARZAN'S QUEST (ERB, Inc., 1936); TARZAN AND THE CITY OF GOLD (ERB, Inc., 1938); TARZAN AND THE FORBIDDEN CITY (ERB, Inc., 1938); TARZAN AND "THE FOREIGN LEGION" (ERB, Inc., 1947); TARZAN THE MAGNIFICENT, TARZAN AND THE MADMAN, TARZAN AND THE CASTAWAYS (published posthumously, Ballantine Books, 1964).

3. Zingg, *supra* note 1, *passim*.

4. Ibid.
5. MALSON and Zingg, *supra* note 1, *passim.*
6. Itard, *The Wild Boy of Aveyron* (1799–1806), trans. *in* MALSON, *supra* note 1, at 91.) *See also* F. TRUFFAUT AND J. GRUAULT, THE WILD CHILD (screenplay, trans. Lewin and Lemery 1973).
7. MALSON, *supra* note 1, at 37.
8. White, *The Forms of Wildness: Archeology of an Idea, in* DUDLEY AND NOVAK, *supra* note 1, at 3, 7.
9. Miner, *The Wild Man through the Looking Glass, in* DUDLEY AND NOVAK, *supra* note 1, at 87, 96–97.
10. Thorslev, *The Wild Man's Revenge, in* DUDLEY AND NOVAK, *supra* note 1, at 281, 282.
11. D. DEFOE, THE LIFE AND STRANGE SURPRISING ADVENTURES OF ROBINSON CRUSOE (originally published in 1719); J. WYSS, THE SWISS FAMILY ROBINSON (1981 ed.); M. SHELLEY, FRANKENSTEIN (1965 ed.); CHATEAUBRIAND, ATALA & RENE, (trans. Cobb 1961).
12. R. KIPLING, THE JUNGLE BOOKS (1961 ed.).
13. Ibid., in Afterword by Cunliffe.
14. Ibid., *passim.*
15. Ibid., at 16.
16. Ibid., at 71–72.
17. LORD RAGLAN, THE HERO/A STUDY IN TRADITION, MYTH AND DRAMA (1956, 1975 ed.).
18. *See* note 59 and accompanying text and G. ESSOE, TARZAN OF THE MOVIES (1968), *passim.*
19. R. LUPOFF, EDGAR RICE BURROUGHS: MASTER OF ADVENTURE (1965); R. FENTON, THE BIG SWINGERS/A BIOGRAPHY 1967); I. PORGES, EDGAR RICE BURROUGHS/THE MAN WHO CREATED TARZAN (1975); E. HOLTSMARK, TARZAN AND TRADITION/CLASSICAL MYTH IN POPULAR LITERATURE (1981); E. HOLTSMARK, EDGAR RICE BURROUGHS (1986).
20. G. MCWHORTER, BURROUGHS DICTIONARY (1987).
21. PORGES, *supra* note 19, *passim.*
22. Burroughs, *Entertainment Is Fiction's Business, reprinted in* 13 GRIDLEY WAVE 3 (January 1964).
23. PORGES, *supra* note 19, *passim.*
24. Ibid., at 322.
25. Ibid., *passim.*
26. Ibid., at 503.
27. Ibid., at 504.
28. Ibid., at 508.
29. Except for the reference to the materials in note 30, *infra,* this discussion of Burroughs's characterization of Tarzan is drawn from the author's study of the character over a period of some thirty years.

30. Slate, *Edgar Rice Burroughs and the Heroic Epic,* 3 RIVERSIDE QUARTERLY 118 (March 1968) *Also see* RAGLAN, *supra* note 17.
31. LUPOFF, *supra* note 19, at 152–153.
32. PORGES, *supra* note 19, at 382 and HOLTSMARK (1986), *supra* note 19, at 10.
33. PORGES, *supra* note 19, at 382.
34. Ibid., at 359.
35. Ibid., at 388.
36. Ibid., at 342.
37. Ibid., at 399–400.
38. Ibid., at 453–454; 757, note 26.
39. Ibid., at 489–490.
40. Ibid., at 492.
41. Ibid., at 421–422.
42. HOLTSMARK (1986), *supra* note 19, at 33.
43. PORGES, *supra* note 19, at 270–274.
44. Ibid., at 509.
45. Ibid., at 510.
46. Ibid., at 441.
47. Ibid., at 510–515.
48. Ibid., at 750, note 38.
49. Ibid., at 316.
50. Milligan, *The First Authentic History of Tarzana,* 15 GRIDLEY WAVE 4 (1964).
51. Coriell, *In* 15 GRIDLEY WAVE 4 (1964).
52. ESSOE, *supra* note 18, at 203.
53. Ex parte O.D. Taragin & Brothers, 68 U.S.P Q. 153 (Dec. Comm'r Pat. 1946).
54. Weitzenkorn v. Lesser, 97 U.S.P.Q. 545 (Cal. Sup. Ct. 1953).
55. 97 U.S.P.Q. at 550.
56. Ibid.
57. 97 U.S.P.Q. at 552.
58. 97 U.S.P.Q. at 554–555. The dissent expressly places Tarzan in the public domain!
59. *See, e.g.,* Abramson, *Art Buchwald Says Eddie Murphy Stole His Idea for a Movie,* WALL. ST. J., November 21, 1988, at 1.
60. Edgar Rice Burroughs v. Charlton Publications, 145 U.S.P.Q. 655 (S.D. N.Y. 1965).
61. 145 U.S.P.Q. at 655. (Second ellipses in original.)
62. Burroughs v. Metro-Goldwyn-Mayer, 210 U.S.P.Q. 579 (S.D. N.Y. 1980), at page 581.
63. Burroughs v. Metro-Goldwyn-Mayer, 683 F.2d 610 (2d Cir. 1982).

64. Burroughs v. Metro-Goldwyn-Mayer, 130 U.S.P.Q. 245 (Cal. Super. Ct. 1961).

65. *See* ESSOE, *supra* note 18, at 151–154.

66. 130 U.S.P.Q. at 245.

67. 130 U.S.P.Q. at 246.

68. Burroughs v. Metro-Goldwyn-Mayer, 135 U.S.P.Q. 40 (Cal. Dist. Ct. App. 1962).

69. 135 U.S.P.Q. at 43.

70. 210 U.S.P.Q. at 579.

71. Burroughs v. Metro-Goldwyn-Mayer, 215 U.S.P.Q. 37 (S.D. N.Y. 1981).

72. 215 U.S.P.Q. at 40. (Brackets in original.)

73. 683 F.2d at 610.

74. 683 F.2d at 621, note 11.

75. 683 F.2d at 632, note 3.

76. 683 F.2d at 624.

77. Edgar Rice Burroughs v. Manns Theatres, 195 U.S.P.Q. 159 (C.D. Cal 1976).

78. 195 U.S.P.Q. at 162.

8

Right of Publicity and Merchandising: Additional Protection for Fictional Characters?

The right of publicity is a form of protection attaching to certain persona under highly specific circumstances of limited interest in the context of fictional characters. The property ordinarily attaches to a celebrity or other public figure or to an individual who is otherwise newsworthy. Rarely does the right of publicity attach to an independent (fictional) persona created by an actor or other performer or accepted as a "signature" of such a celebrity.

Clayton Moore's continued assumption of the persona of the Lone Ranger is a case in point never subjected to judicial analysis. (*see* chapter 6.) Dracula, as personified by Bela Lugosi, is the principle example of such a created character examined by the judicial system. The Marx Brothers represent a kind of transition between real persons and fictional persona. Just how successfully these unique persona have been protected will be considered here.

The right of publicity is of interest in terms of fictional characters as a conceptual bridge between the basic protection of intellectual properties in literary and the performance media and the protection of characters in their merchandise incarnations. The cases in point, however, focus primarily on alienation of the property rather than on its existence in the first instance.

Of greater pertinence in the context of this work is the contemporary merchandising phenomenon alluded to from time to time in the course of discussions of copyright, trademark, and unfair competition. In this chapter parallel protection of characters carried beyond the literary and performance media will be addressed in some detail. These are cases where neither the character nor the protection stops with the written, graphic, or dynamic presentations. Once again the crucial interplay among copyright, trademark, unfair competition, and between these properties and contract law will be illustrated.

RIGHT OF PUBLICITY

The Concept of a Personal Right of Publicity

The so-called right of publicity was first recognized in an article of the ninteenth century.[1] Evolving from principles of copyright and contract, the novel right was conceived from the proposition "that property in its widest sense could . . . encompass the right to an inviolate personality, [which] extended" from accepted privacy and property rights.[2] Once recognized, the right underwent the usual judicial alterations. Specifically, the right to name and likeness became a part of the more general right of privacy. As a personal right, publicity died with the individual, and at least one court held it to be nonassignable.

Actually the raison d'être of the right of publicity is in its transferability, which may be active or passive—if accepted at all. Another open question is that of duration. Is the right of publicity limited or unlimited in duration? While real property is infinite—it never ceases to exist as property—copyright is finite—it ceases to exist in a fixed time frame by operation of law. (Trademark, presumably, has the potential for infinite life but can be rendered finite, as was established in chapter 4.) The question of duration of a right to publicity has yet to be answered in court, but it is noted that "[n]ames and likenesses are symbols, one linguistic and the other pictorial, which represent the subject party and his connotative impact."[3] The right of publicity, then, sounds like trademark joined with something approaching copyright's expression.

The first case to recognize a right of publicity is founded in breach of contract.[4] A baseball player granted to the plaintiff exclusive rights to use his photograph in association with its brand of chewing gum. The defendant, a rival of the plaintiff, induced the ballplayer to enter a comparable contract for use of his photograph. The defendant argued that there was no actionable wrong, because the player had done no more than grant a release from liability. The Second Circuit disagreed, because the contract went further.

The exclusivity of the right granted rendered it property rather than merely the release of a personal right to privacy. The inducement to enter a second contract constituted tortious behavior. The Second Circuit expressly recognized an independent right of publicity (reflecting the value of the photograph) dissociated from the right to privacy. A pecuniary interest was recognized in the use of the photograph. Interestingly enough, this particular property may prove to be resistant to defenses analogous to fair use or to a First Amendment defense—to which copyright and trademark are vulnerable—and, further, public interest may not be a judicial consideration.[5]

Nearly thirty years later the need to distinguish the right of publicity from rights comprising invasion of privacy was reiterated.[6] Invasion of privacy was said to include commercial misappropriation of one's name or likeness. This wrong is attended by an injury to the individual's personal feelings along with economic injury, the latter leading to measurable damages. The capacity to take action on this wrong does not survive the individual, as is illustrated by cases involving the families of Al Capone and Jesse James. That capacity dies with the person in question because there can no longer be injury to the feelings of the person.

On the other hand, the right of publicity protects the person in question from appropriations for the taker's direct commercial advantage. Because the right is intended to reward the holder for the market value associated with his name or likeness, it becomes a property right through commercial exploitation. As a property, that right, then, is both alienable and perpetual.[7]

Celebrities and Other Personages

Martin Luther King, Jr. In fact, only one case has been found where state law recognized both the existence of the right of publicity and its survival of the subject—and that without commercial exploitation during the subject's lifetime.[8] Significantly, the public figure was Martin Luther King, Jr., who was neither a public official nor an entertainer. Thus, even though King is clearly a public figure, the case is more reminiscent of invasion of privacy than right of publicity as proffered in the previous cases, which may have been a primary consideration to the Georgia Supreme Court.

Nancy Sinatra. In the late sixties the right of publicity took a step toward recognition as an independent intellectual property, thanks to the popularity of Nancy Sinatra's hit "These Boots Are Made for Walkin'."[9] The defendants described a line of tires as "wide boots" and advertised the line with the music and revised lyrics of Sinatra's hit. The singer remained unseen, but her voice was not unlike that of the original. The unsuccessful suit was based in unfair competition pursuant to state law.

Sinatra was claiming that she had popularized the song to the extent that her name was identified with it. Further, she was best known in connection with it and it had attained secondary meaning. Her voice and style were being deliberately imitated with intent to deceive the public. The impression conveyed was that she was participating, despite the lack of any contract with her. The defendants countered that the imitation was insufficient to support a cause of action.

In fact there was a series of comparable commercials involving the "voices" of Aunt Jemima, Alastair Sim, Bert Lahr, and the Fifth Dimension. Denial of summary judgment was affirmed, at least in part upon the finding of no competition between Nancy Sinatra and Goodyear.[10]

Elvis Presley. Elvis Presley almost succeeded in protecting his commercial rights where others had failed.[11] During his lifetime, Presley formed Boxcar Enterprises, Inc. to which he assigned all rights to use his name and likeness for commercial purposes. After Elvis died, Boxcar transferred these rights to the plaintiff, Factors. The defendant, Pro Arts, marketed a poster from a photograph of Elvis to which it owned the copyright. When suit was entered, the question of survival was entered as a defense and rejected at trial. On appeal, applying Tennessee law, it was yet again held that the right of publicity, even when exercised, does not survive the subject's death.

Johnny Carson. With reference to "The World's Foremost Commodian," Here's Johnny Portable Toilets, Inc. moved into marketing, only to be met with a lawsuit.[12] Johnny Carson's theories were unfair competition and invasion of the right of privacy, with reference to the right of publicity. The former was rejected for lack of any likelihood of confusion. The latter was also rejected since neither Carson's name nor his likeness was being exploited. Dismissal on both grounds was affirmed.

From these illustrative cases, there is every reason to believe that where celebrity or notoriety is the basis of any claim to right of publicity, that legal protection is actually more theoretical than real. But what of fictional or partially fictional characters?

Cher. Sometimes it is difficult to discern where the performer ends and the performance persona begins. The foregoing celebrities appear to be straightforward entertainers who are marketing a mild extension of their actual personalities. With Cher there is an aura of the fictional in her performance: She has been described as a "well-known entertainer who performs under the name 'Cher.' "[13] When the flamboyant entertainer was dissatisfied with an interview, she took legal steps to prevent its appearance in print. Despite her efforts it was published, and Cher sued on a number of grounds. Significantly none was defamation or invasion of privacy; two counts were of misappropriation—of her name and likeness and of her right to publicity. She proved her case and was awarded both general and punitive damages. On appeal Cher was only slightly less successful.

The Ninth Circuit found the right of publicity to be increasingly limited in California in deference to First Amendment rights. Thus the judgment against one defendant was reversed.[14] A second publication, however, engaged in explicit promotion using Cher's name and photograph. Further, this defendant conveyed the false impression that she had given them exclusive material. The impression on the public was one of endorsement. Significantly, the Ninth Circuit observed, "[a]dvertising to promote a news medium . . . is not actionable under an appropriation of publicity theory so long as the advertising does not falsely claim that the public figure endorses that news medium."[15] Here the claim that Cher had "told" defendant anything was patently false. The First Amendment will not protect such falsehood, and both the lower court's ruling and damages were upheld. In a few short pages, the Ninth Circuit's opinion illustrated the array of intellectual properties associated with personality or character. This particular case combines right of publicity with a suggestion of trademark reasoning.

Dracula, the Sheik, and Other Roles

Dracula. Shortly after the Cher case, Dracula followed lesser personages into defeat.[16] In 1930 an agreement had been entered for the production of the film, *Dracula.* It contained the provision ultimately in point.

> "The producer shall have the right to . . . *exploit in connection with* the said photoplay any and all of the artist's acts, poses, plays and appearances of any and all kinds hereunder, and *shall further have the right to record, reproduce, transmit, exhibit, distribute, and exploit in connection with* said photoplay the artist's voice. . . . The producer shall likewise have the right to use and give publicity to the *artist's name and likeness.*"[17]

Through the years a number of actors have portrayed Dracula in a number of Universal Pictures films, but it was Bela Lugosi who became identified with the role and whose likeness was used in merchandising. When Lugosi died in 1956, his widow and son claimed that they had inherited certain rights of publicity not included in the referenced provision. They asserted appropriation of those rights by Universal from 1960 on. The issues, then, were whether Lugosi had retained any rights and, if so, whether they survived his death and descended to the plaintiffs. The trial court agreed with the plaintiffs' contention that Bela Lugosi's Dracula persona was the specific property subject to licensing. The actor was found to have possessed a proprietary right in that persona, which did not terminate with his death.

In reversing, the California Supreme Court commenced with the individual's right of privacy, with reference to the four personal rights, one of which is the right of publicity.[18] None of these personal rights, according to the high court, extends to members of the proprietor's family and none is assignable. The right to exploit them, however, is assignable.

Although Lugosi had enjoyed the right to exploit his "right of publicity" as well as the independent right to restrain others from doing so, he had never availed himself of either. The right to do so, that is, to create a business, product, or service, does not survive. Because Lugosi himself had not exploited his rights, his heirs could not do so.

Thus, in California at least, the right of publicity is recognized, not as property, but as a personal right.[19] As such it can be initially exploited only by the original proprietor, who is the persona in question. If this individual dies without exploiting the persona, his or her right is extinguished. In essence, the persona is in the public domain until another utilizes it in creating a business product or service. This particular situation would be analogous more to trademark than to copyright.

A concurring opinion distinguished the relationship between Lugosi—the actor—and Dracula—the role—from two other situations that are themselves legally distinguishable despite inviting comparison: on the one hand Groucho Marx, for example, "played himself" on screen; on the other, Red Skelton, Abbott and Costello, and Laurel and Hardy all created characters. The implication is that, because they were the creators of the persona in question, only the latter personalities would have had proprietary rights. Lugosi merely acted what another created. He had no more proprietary right in the Dracula character than actors portraying Hamlet in some remarkably unique way have in the Prince of Denmark.

A major dissenting opinion commenced not from the specified right of privacy but from some other unspecified, heritable interest which, the opinion asserted, was violated by Universal to the extent the licensing efforts exceeded its contractual rights.

Rudolf Valentino, "the Sheik." The Lugosi case was cited as controlling in a similar situation raised by an alleged nephew of the late Rudolf Valentino.[20] The action arose from a fictionalized account of the matinee idol's life.

The Green Hornet. Not much later something akin to right of publicity surfaced again.[21] The former radio hero, the purely fictional Green Hornet, was the subject. The lawsuit sought to restrain the use of his name on buttons merchandising the more recent television version of the hero. The buttons superimposed the legend "Official Member Super Hero Hornet Society" over a drawing of a green hornet. The court agreed with the plaintiff's assertion that the buttons were calculated to deceive the public with regard to their origin. The defendant in fact had been an unsuccessful bidder for this particular merchandising license. While akin to the right of publicity, this purely fictional persona, without reference to the actor portraying him, is subject to trademark without falling into the right of publicity issue as such. The parallels, however, are present.

Special Cases

Wyatt Earp. Without use of the phrase "right of publicity," one case represents bridges to this property right from trademark and from trademark into merchandising.[22] Based on unfair competition and trademark infringement, Wyatt Earp Enterprises sued a manufacturer of children's clothes who was merchandising under the name, mark, and symbol "Wyatt Earp." The proprietor of the Wyatt Earp mark was the producer of the television series *Life and Legend of Wyatt Earp,* which presented a fictionalized version of the historical figure.

Although the defendant had been a licensee of the name, it continued usage after the license expired and was granted to another. Pursuant to trademark law, the plaintiff asserted that the character name had acquired "secondary meaning." The court's rather exasperated observation in this regard reveals much of the marketing blitz so often associated with a character who touches the American imagination.

Responding to a motion for injunction *pendente lite,* the court railed that the name of the fictionalized personage had been battered into the public consciousness by the television program to an extent far beyond any fame or notoriety of the man himself. From its inception the program was among the most popular in the nation. Weekly transcontinental broadcasts of the popular program generated enormous publicity throughout the mass media. Thus, the court found as a preliminary matter that the name and characterization of Wyatt Earp as televised by the plaintiff had become identified in the mind of the public with merchandise upon which the name was imprinted. Further, this identification and goodwill extended to the field of children's clothes distributed under that name, mark, and symbol. Finally, the defendant was merchandising the Wyatt Earp clothing as such because of popular demand for merchandise identified with the program and the plaintiff.[23]

The injunction was granted. Even though the parties were not in direct competition, consumer confusion was held to be likely because of the striking resemblance between the properties. Note that had the actor, himself, been the party to this case, right of publicity might have been specifically in issue. Actually, the legal successors to Wyatt Earp himself might have enjoyed rights with regard to the television series and the resultant merchandising, as noted in the next case or as flowing from the California statute referenced thereafter.

The Marx Brothers. The case involving Groucho Marx came before the federal courts in New York.[24] Contrary to California law, that of New York recognizes an inheritable right of publicity. The subject matter of the suit was a successful musical, *A Day in Hollywood/A Night in the Ukraine,* that made satiric comment on the Hollywood of the thirties. The Ukraine portion dealt with how the Marx brothers might have dramatized Chekhov's novel, *The Bear.* Although the comedians' names were not used, their appearance and comedic style were.

The plaintiffs sought damages in the nature of a licensing fee, arguing that the exhibition was in derogation of their exclusive rights of publicity, specifically that associated with commercialization of Groucho, Chico, and Harpo. The trial court granted the plaintiffs a partial summary judgment on the basis of New York law, but the appellate court, applying California law, reversed on the basis that rights of publicity do not survive. Reference was made to both the Dracula and the Valentino cases.

With reference to the former, the court considered possible interpretations. The first was trademark, which could protect what the celebrity brought to the product (character) in question during his lifetime. The other interpretation depended on a product or service promoted during the creator's lifetime apart from trademark. The elements of neither interpretation could be met by the plaintiffs representing Groucho and his brothers. It would appear that the Second Circuit agreed with the concurring justice in California: the Marx Brothers were deemed not to be characters in the sense intended here.

The California Response

In recent years California has taken legislative steps to nullify the defeat of claims raised in the Dracula case.[25] In addition to California Civil Code 3344, which protects against the use of a living person's name, photograph or likeness, the more recent section 990 provides that the right of publicity is a property right that is freely transferable without a prerequisite for merchandising. The duration question is also answered with the proviso that no action can be sustained for an unauthorized use occurring more than fifty years after the personality's death.

MERCHANDISING OF CHARACTERS

Arguably, the Lone Ranger is one of the most effectively and widely merchandised characters ever.[26] A coloring book was still being published in the early eighties. This popularity, however, can imply, if not actually generate, legal problems.

As with Tarzan, elements of the Lone Ranger's world have run the risk of becoming somewhat too familiar.

Some of the elements of the Lone Ranger's world have become cliches, still in use in the eighties. Reportedly a television script written early in this decade referred to a close friend as being a "Tonto." In response the friend reciprocated with a reference to "Kemo Sabe." Both terms remain household words signifying friendship or companionship.[27] The legal question is whether cliches are generic. Quite obviously the marketplace can become saturated in more than the advertising sense, but the merchandising of characters proceeds apace—as do the related lawsuits.

Toys and Games

In February of 1977 the Director of Public Affairs for Twentieth Century-Fox wrote to Ideal Toy Corp.[28] The letter, announcing the upcoming release of *Star Wars,* solicited Ideal's attendance at a presentation scheduled for the annual toy fair. Ideal, not unlike certain others, declined to attend, claiming no interest. Science fiction films are chancy—as are films themselves—as merchandising properties, in large part because of the frequently short release life. *Star Wars* was dismissed as rather an ordinary property, the elements of which had been done before.[29]

Star Wars was released in May of 1977. The rest is cinematic history. In less than seven months, *Star Wars* became the most financially successful movie to date. Some 20 licenses to *Star Wars* products had been issued since the end of 1976, but none to Ideal.

Ideal began a reevaluation. It took into account the critical acclaim and instant popularity of *Star Wars,* added the continued popularity of *Star Trek* along with the publicity then surrounding the space shuttle, took note of imminent release of more space movies, and observed the space toys its competitors were turning out.[30]

As a result of this evaluation, Ideal attempted to revise old product lines to expedite distribution. One Zogg became Zeroid and JJ Armes turned into Zem 21. In need of a villain, Ideal turned out Knight of Darkness and dressed him all in black. A ship by the name of Star Hawk joined them.

The modified creatures were challenged as too close to R2–D2, C–3PO, and Darth Vader. Ideal therefore sought a declaration that its "Star Team" did not infringe *Star Wars*. Kenner, which had not yet brought out its own *Star Wars* line but was issuing "Early Bird Certificates," sued on copyright infringement and cross-claimed for injunctive relief, arguing copyright on a dramatic work extending to characters—given certain circumstances.[31]

As a starting point, there was no doubt that Ideal was seeking to make use of the themes embodied in the three original characters. But theme, an idea, is not protected; it merely stands behind its protectable expression. The issue, then, starts with the cinematic characters and turns to their toy counterparts, the true subjects of the legal claim.

> The characters from "Star Wars" are elements in a drama; they have "character" because they are part of a plot in which they interact with each other. Thus, they have attributes which are suggested by the movie itself. The toys have no such qualities as they exist in their basic, copyrighted form. The child who plays with them will give them certain qualities, but these will be the creation of the child and not of Ideal. Thus, any comparison will have to be made solely on the basis of physical appearance; in other words, the *sole* attribute of the dolls will have to be compared to only *one* attribute of the movie characters.[32]

That factor, in addition to a variety of difficulties in comparing within and across media, led the district court to find insufficient similarity to support injunctive relief. Moreover, the court recognized Ideal's intent to capitalize on the *Star Wars* phenomenon but took special note of its efforts to avoid copying. A further reason, then, for denying injunctive relief arose out of objective evidence of independent creation (which will even overcome substantial similarity where the latter does exist).

In denying injunctive relief, the court characterized as "mistaken" Kenner's contention that *Star Wars* was the source of Ideal's toys. The court further held that there was no appropriation of any clear symbol and that Kenner was unlikely to succeed in demonstrating an attempt to mislead, thus crossing from copyright into trademark protection.

E.T. The Extraterrestrial followed in the footsteps of *Star Wars*, both in popularity and in the launching of lawsuits. Like *Star Wars* before it, this film was extraordinarily popular and financially successful.[33] Both the film and the central character acquired tremendous—and valuable—goodwill. That character became identified with the studio and their film and launched a licensing business, both large and valuable. This business included "soft-sculpture" dolls.[34]

The defendant's doll, designed after the film had been viewed, was marketed as "The Visitor from Outer Space" and "The Creature from Outer Space." This doll was registered as a trademark in August of 1982. In September of 1982 J.A.R. was notified that it was infringing. The plaintiff, Universal, applied for a preliminary injunction on two bases: copyright infringement and violation of the Lanham Act. The district court found the idea of the two dolls substantially similar. In fact, according to this California district:

> The character "E.T." in the motion picture . . . contains unique elements of expression and is protectable under the Copyright Act. . . . The expression of the idea of the character "E.T." in the motion picture, . . . [plaintiffs' dolls], and the defendants' dolls is substantially similar under the intrinsic "ordinary observer" test of Krofft. . . . In addition, the total concept and feel of defendants' dolls is the same as the character "E.T." in the copyrighted motion picture and as the copyrighted . . . dolls.[35]

The properties were compared in detail and then the court held that the plaintiffs were likely also to succeed on the trademark claim. Confusion among the public as to source and sponsorship was likely. Hence, Universal was entitled to a preliminary injunction, and J.A.R.'s imposters were impounded to be held in trust while trial proceeded.[36]

That marketing of popular characters can reel out of control is demonstrated in the form of additional E.T. surrogates:

> In order to maintain a consistent image and appeal for the "E.T." character consonent with that development in the movie, Steven Spiel-

berg, who directed the movie and who is responsible, in large part, for its creation and success, has retained and exercises personal control over the nature and quality of all "E.T." items to be marketed.[37]

Toys are in essence sculptures. In one case involving two manufacturers of toys, the plaintiff was seeking a declaratory judgment that there was no violation of the rights of its competitor.[38] The defendant counterclaimed on the basis of copyright infringement. Because the defendant's toys were derivative (of Walt Disney properties) they were entitled to copyright protection only to the extent that the toys' original aspects were more than trivial. Here there was no originality, and the defendant was precluded from establishing the case for infringement. The appellate court observed that slight differences between works will not preclude a finding of infringement where there is substantial similarity but that numerous differences can undercut that essential finding of similarity in the first instance. Aesthetic impact is a transcendent factor of concern.

There are some interesting twists in a second case involving toys where the trial court's refusal to issue a preliminary injunction was affirmed.[39] Mattel sued Remco on a variety of theories, including copyright infringement, trademark infringement, and common law unfair competition, with the contention that the latter's Warlord toys were copies of the former's Masters of the Universe. It is worth reviewing the court's own observations in finding for the defendant:

Remco gave its sculptor a Mattel doll to show him what kind of doll it wanted, and to insure that Remco's doll would not appear to be the physically weaker of the two toys. But the district court apparently credited the evidence of Remco's expert on human anatomy that the Remco doll was not a direct copy of the Mattel doll, but rather was simply another artist's rendering of the human form with an exaggerated musculature. The artist who sculpted the model for the Remco figure had body-building and comic magazines as well as other material from which he worked.

Though the dolls' bodies are very similar, nearly all the similarity can be attributed to the fact that both are artist's renderings of the same unprotectable idea—a superhuman muscleman crouching in what since Neanderthal times has been a traditional fighting pose.[40]

Mattel ... was at the time of ... hearing, already selling as many "Masters of the Universe" dolls as it can produce, and for inadequately explained reasons it delayed bringing this action until just before the start of the Christmas selling season. The district court therefore correctly concluded that an injunction would hurt Remco more than it would help Mattel.[41]

These observations at the very least reveal just how disingenuous toy manufacturers are and, further, just how astute the courts can be. From only a few sentences one can infer a multitude of insights.

Computerized images. In this modern age of electronic games there is a new medium for copyright infringement.[42] In fact it might be said that Pac-Man has sued K. C. Munchkin.[43] Plaintiff Atari appealed the denial of its motion for a preliminary injunction in a case based on copyright infringement and unfair competition, the latter pursuant to Illinois law.

The developers of K. C. Munchkin had unsuccessfully sought the license for home videos of Pac-Man. Upon completing the K. C. Munchkin program, the buyer concluded it was totally different from Pac-Man, but customers and their sales staff in fact relied heavily on the comparison of the two. Citing minimal protection for games, the appellate court set about a determination of substantial similarity in the narrow sense of scènes à faire or whether the games extended beyond that unprotected area into expression subject to copyright.

The court favored the issues with a particularly careful analysis demonstrating a certain empathy for the medium:

To assess the impact of certain differences, one factor to consider is the nature of the protected material and the setting in which it appears. Video games, unlike an artist's painting or even other audiovisual works, appeal to an audience that is fairly undiscriminating insofar as their concern about more subtle differences in artistic expression. The main attraction of a game such as PAC-MAN lies in the stimulation provided by the intensity of the competition. A person who is entranced by the play of the game "would be disposed to overlook" many of the minor differences in detail and "regard their aesthetic appeal as the same."[44]

The court reversed the lower court and ordered entry of the preliminary injunction sought by Atari with the observation that the dissimilarities raised by defendants only served to emphasize the extent of the deliberate copy. These similarities outweighed the questionable differences. It is important to note, as did the court, the relatively short life span of a video game. This and other decisions tend to favor the plaintiffs where the popularity of their works is likely to be short lived. One suspects that under comparable circumstances, a novel is less likely to be protected because of its greater life expectancy (if not because of its more discriminating public).

IMPLICATIONS FOR CHARACTERS IN COURT

The foregoing discussions have revealed just how serious the protection of characters can be in the marketplace and suggest that no court should lightly dismiss characters in the popular media as too trivial to be deserving of careful reasoning under one or more legal theory. The Batman craze of the summer of 1989 is further proof the characters are to be taken quite seriously indeed.[45] Should further proof be needed, language from a recent article about Shamu, "the" killer whale, is compelling—and misleading:

> In the booming theme park business, success requires a cast of identifiable characters amenable to marketing. And if millions know Shamu now, just wait till the trademarked character falls into the hands of whoever is about to pay a mint for her. . . . [W]hat the buyers really are after is Shamu—and the potential to take the lucrative, lovable character overseas. (*Shamu actually is not one but several whales that perform under the name, a sort of Sea World generic.*) . . . Shamu . . . is an indispensable character of the sort that can be used to entertain visitors . . . and to grace marketing blitzes. . . . Disney['s] Chairman . . . says the use of characters isn't just an aspect of the company, "that is all our company is. We are nothing else." . . . Disney, of course, remains the undisputed master of character creation and exploitation, having parleyed its animated images into $4 billion a year in revenue. . . . Universal . . . hopes to capitalize on such popular characters as "E.T." and the shark from "Jaws."[46]

Characters, in fact, have been largely overlooked by the commentators both as a significant property and as a model for examining judicial reasoning on copyright, trademark, and related intellectual properties. In the final chapter, the case law addressing copyright in characters will be reconciled and a model for predicting the outcome of future cases will be proferred.

NOTES

1. *See* Ginsburg, *Transfer of the Right of Publicity: Dracula's Progeny and Privacy's Stepchild,* 25 COPYRIGHT L. SYMP. (ASCAP) 1 (1980). The referenced article is Warren and Brandeis, *The Right to Privacy,* 4 HARV. L. REV. 193 (1890).

2. Ginsburg, *supra* note 1, at 6.

3. *Id., passim,* 30. This commentator calls for a finite existence more in keeping with copyright concepts.

4. Haelen Laboratories v. Topps Chewing Gum, 202 F.2d 866 (2d Cir. 1953); *cert. den.* 346 U.S. 816 (1953).

5. *See* Phillips, *A Haystack in a Hurricane: A Divergent Case Law on the Right of Publicity and the Copyright Act of 1976,* 63 J. PAT. OFF. SOC'Y 296 (1981). *But see* note 14 *infra* and accompanying text.

6. Rader, *The "Right of Publicity"—A New Dimension,* 61 J. PAT. OFF. SOC'Y 228 (1979).

7. Ibid., at 229.

8. Martin Luther King, Jr. Center v. Amer. Heritage Products, 216 U.S.P.Q. 711 (Ga. Sup. Ct. 1982).

9. Sinatra v. Goodyear Tire & Rubber Co., 435 F.2d 711 (9th Cir. 1970).

10. The matter of imitations of popular singers for commercials has peaked at the close of the eighties. Reportedly the New York district has refused to dismiss Bette Midler's action, breaking new ground in this area. *See* Schmitt, *Singers Get Green Light to Sue Imitators,* WALL ST. J., August 19, 1988, at 13.

11. Factors, Etc. v. Pro Arts, 652 F.2d 278 (2d Cir. 1981). Elvis merchandisers, like the late celebrity's fans, never say die. *See* Smith, *Elvis Merchandisers Are All Shook up by a Federal Lawsuit,* WALL ST. J., June 30, 1988, at 1.

12. Carson v. Here's Johnny Portable Toilets, 698 F.2d 831 (6th Cir. 1983). The case was also reported by BNA with reference to

plaintiffs "flushed with indignation." 25 PAT. TRADEMARK & COPYRIGHT J. 329 (February 17, 1983).

13. Cher v. Forum International, 217 U.S.P.Q. 407 (9th Cir. 1982), at 408.

14. 217 U.S.P.Q. 409.

15. 217 U.S.P.Q. 410.

16. Lugosi v. Universal Pictures, 205 U.S.P.Q. 1090 (Cal. Sup. Ct. 1979). The Supreme Court adopted as its own the opinion of the appellate court.

17. *See* 205 U.S.P.Q. at 1092–1093, note 2 (Emphasis in original).

18. The others are the rights to be free from (1) intrusions into one's seclusion or solitude, (2) public disclosures of embarrassing private facts and (3) appropriation of one's name or likeness for the advantage of the appropriating party.

19. *But see* text accompanying note 25 *infra*.

20. Guglielmi v. Spelling-Goldberg Productions, 205 U.S.P.Q. 1116 (Cal. Sup. Ct. 1979).

21. American Broadcasting Co. v. Button World Mfg., 151 U.S.P.Q. 361 (N.Y. Sup. Ct. 1966).

22. Wyatt Earp Enterprises v. Sackman, 116 U.S.P.Q. 122 (S.D. N.Y. 1958).

23. 116 U.S.P.Q. at 123–124.

24. Groucho Marx Productions v. Day and Night Co., 689 F.2d 317 (2d Cir. 1982).

25. *See* Rohde, *Dracula, Still Undead (Unresolved Right-of-Publicity Questions Are Sure to Haunt the Courts)*, *in* 1985 ENTERTAINMENT, PUBLISHING AND THE ARTS HANDBOOK (J. D. Viera and M. Meyer, eds.).

26. D. ROTHEL, WHO WAS THAT MASKED MAN?/THE STORY OF THE LONE RANGER(TM) (rev. ed. 1981), *passim*.

27. *Id.*, at 192.

28. Ideal Toy Corp. v. Kenner Products Div., 197 U.S.P.Q. 738 (S.D. N.Y. 1977).

29. 197 U.S.P.Q. at 741.

30. Ibid.

31. 197 U.S.P.Q. at 743–744.

32. 197 U.S.P.Q. at 747 (Emphasis in original, footnote omitted).

33. Universal Studios v. J.A.R. Sales, 216 U.S.P.Q. 679 (C.D. Cal. 1982).

34. 216 U.S.P.Q. 679, *passim*.

35. 216 U.S.P.Q. at 681.

36. 216 U.S.P.Q. at 684. "Merchandising has become so important

a market that a journal dedicated to the phenomenon was initiated in 1982. *Merchandising Reporter* devotes each issue to a central theme of merchandising of sports—or character licensing." *Licensing Huckleberry Hound, Yogi Bear, and the Flintstones.* 69 A.B.A. J. 983 (1983).

For more on the interplay of copyright and trademark in the context of merchandising, *see* Battersby and Grimes, *Protecting Merchandising Properties under Copyright Law, in* 1985 ENTERTAINMENT, PUBLISHING AND THE ARTS HANDBOOK (J. D. Viera and M. Meyer, eds.).

37. Universal Studios v. Kamar Industries, 217 U.S.P.Q. 1163 (S.D. Tex. 1982), at 1164.

38. Durham Industries v. Tomy Corp, 630 F.2d 905 (2d Cir. 1980).

39. Mattel v. Azrack-Hamway International, 221 U.S.P.Q. 302 (2d Cir. 1983).

40. 221 U.S.P.Q. at 304.

41. 221 U.S.P.Q. at 305. *Also see* Conan Properties v. Conans Pizza, 752 F.2d 145 (5th Cir. 1985).

42. The cases addressing copyright and other intellectual properties associated with computers and computer programs are well beyond the scope of this work.

43. Atari v. North American, Etc., 672 F.2d 607 (7th Cir. 1982).

44. 672 F.2d at 619.

45. *See, e.g.,* Landro, *Can Bat-Movie Survive All the Bat Items?*, WALL ST. J., June 13, 1989, at Bl; Lambert, *Fake "Bat" Products Spark a Crackdown Far beyond Gotham,* WALL. ST. J., July 21, 1989, at B7. *Also see* Sansweet, *"E.T." Is Coming to Video—But First a Marketing Blitz,* WALL ST. J., May 6, 1988, at 23; Turner, *Will Mickey Get Caught in an Ad Trap?*, WALL ST. J., March 23, 1989, at B1; Karr, *Lively Raisins on TV Are Grapes of Wrath to One Distributor,* WALL ST. J., January 21, 1987, at 1.

There is also a case in the Second Circuit involving the "batcave," arising from allegations of copyright and trademark infringement: DC Comics v. Reel Fantasy, 217 U.S.P.Q. 307 (2d Cir. 1982).

46. Waldman and Turner, *Shamu Is Big Prize Buyer of Sea World Will Get for Its Money,* WALL ST. J., August 28, 1989, at 1 and A2.

9

Copyright and Characters: Reconciliation and Prediction

ANALYSIS OF COPYRIGHT DECISIONS

Neither the copyright statute nor the Lanham Act makes specific, express reference to character or characterization as an independent, protectible entity. Among jurisdictions, the independent copyright protection of characters as such has the appearance of inconsistency, in part because the precise question does not come before the courts with any great frequency. A reasonable inference is that characters, like sequels and derivative works, are thoroughly addressed in licensing agreements and other contractual arrangements. But the question can arise even if licenses and contracts are thorough. When questions addressing the distribution of rights to use characters arise, the nature of any property in character necessarily per se comes to the fore. The Ninth Circuit does not yet identify that property, which the circuit does recognize, as copyright. The Second Circuit, on the other hand, does identify character as a creature of copyright.

Whatever the identification, for copyright protection to attach, case law requires that the character go beyond a mere idea and rise to the level of expression through development and delineation. Expression here almost certainly consists of some combination of characteristics, actions, and reactions, but no legal formula presently exists for the extraction of protectable expression from the basic underlying idea and scènes à faire. There is no precise theorem fixing the place where the line is to be drawn. The decisions, like all those resolving matters of intellectual property, will be subjective judgment calls.

Trends in the Case Law

At large. Three classes of cases can, nevertheless, be distinguished:

1. Character and work are coextensive and, therefore, inseparable: taking either the work or the character is necessarily infringement of the whole.
2. Character is subordinate to the work; the character is neither separable nor independently protectible.
   a. Taking of the character goes to infringement of the work and
   b. Character protection is encompassed within the copyright of the whole.
3. Character is an integral part of the work but sufficiently delineated to stand independent.
   a. Taking of the character can go to infringement of the work but
   b. Character may also be separately protectible.

Where character has been subject to copyright around the circuits, it has been subordinate to the work or, more frequently, coextensive. Sometimes judicial language suggests something of a transition between the two. Cases are reported from the First, Seventh, and the Fifth Circuits. With only one exception, the characters are at least arguably coextensive with the work and protection attaches or fails on the basis of the standard copyright elements and defenses.

Among the cases are those involving Stella Dallas,[1] Francis the Talking Mule[2] and a prototype of Starman.[3] Two cases address Margaret Mitchell's Scarlett O'Hara and the principal characters of *Gone with the Wind*. In the earlier case, the characters are handled as if coextensive with the work.[4] In the latter, judicial language suggests they are subordinate.[5]

In each case the characters are treated as copyright properties. Whether protection applies depends on standard copyright concepts, particularly defenses such as scènes à faire and parody. It is worth noting parenthetically that Scarlett O'Hara and company had been expressly preserved from the issue raised in the Sam Spade case through express contractual provisions addressing the characters, particularly in the context of retained sequel rights.

In the Second Circuit. New York recognizes copyright in character. Thus the case law in point consists of straightforward copyright analysis. In this circuit most characters seem to be analyzed as if coextensive with the work. Others are clearly subordinate. No character is treated as an independent property.

Among those characters the New York courts deemed coextensive are Superman (in his appearances in comics[6] and, possibly, on film[7]), Mutt and Jeff[8] (from printed cartoons), Hopalong Cassidy[9] (in novels and films) and Amos and Andy[10] (in radio and television episodes). In those cases where copyright protection is not found, the holding is based on some combination of dissimilarities in the subject properties, scènes à faire where similarities do exist, the lack of taking of development and delineation, and parody to the extent some taking is found.[11]

In one case it is noted that audiovisual works of television are visual representations equivalent to expression going beyond unprotected word portraits.[12] Early reasoning in this circuit sounded much more like trademark and unfair competition than copyright.[13] The one character treated more as inseparable than the others was also held to have been retained by his creator as a copyright.[14]

Among the characters treated as subordinate to the work, all but one were ensembles. Among the ensembles are the people of WKRP,[15] Indiana Jones and company,[16] Luke Skywalker and company,[17] and the rodeo cowboys of *Stir Crazy*.[18] The loner is none other than Tarzan.[19] Only Tarzan was protected. Significantly, his is the only case in which it is the popular character who is allegedly infringed. In all the others, the plaintiffs are claiming that the popular characters were taken from their lesser-known counterparts. Tarzan is protected through contract rights. The *Star Wars* and *Raiders of the Lost Ark* ensembles were not infringements for lack of substantial similarities or outright dissimilarities. The others were considered scènes à faire or too dissimilar to constitute infringements.

In the Ninth Circuit. Of the characters reported from the Ninth Circuit, Sam Spade is the earliest.[20] He is expressly denied independent copyright identity, but he is recognized as an independent, separable entity in the context of a licensing agreement.

Not surprisingly, the remaining characters subject to analysis in this circuit—with one exception— have all been found to be subordinate to the work. The exception is Regan from *The Exorcist,* where the film was found to be subordinate to the character in denying protection of both.[21] Arguably, the court was implying a situation where the two were actually coextensive.

For the sake of clarification the remaining cases will be analyzed from a chart. (See table 1.) It is the characters for whom copyright protection is not available that are of interest here. What do they have in common? First, they are all represented in the visual media, relatively simple in comparison with the literary media. More significantly, protection is denied on the basis of copyright defenses. Under the circumstances there are no surprises here.

But two of the cases do have surprises, both out of the circuit court itself. In 1983 the Ninth Circuit seemingly ignored the Sam Spade decision in reversing the Central District for a factual determination of whether the *Battlestar Galactica* ensemble infringed that of *Star Wars.*[30] Admittedly, neither group is standing outside its work, but the case does carry an implication of retreat from the language, if not the result, of the Sam Spade case.

In 1988 there was an express suggestion of retreat on the part of the Ninth Circuit.[31] Here the court seems to be reasoning that the only thing precluding a direct reversal of Sam

Table 1
The Ninth Circuit's Treatment of Characters Subordinate to the Work

CHARACTER AT ISSUE	PROTECTION	REASONING	PROTOTYPE/POPULAR CLAIMING (CLAIMANT'S MEDIUM)
H. R. Pufnstuf[22]	YES	Intrinsic test (established)	Popular (TV comm'ls)
E.T.[23]	YES	Intrinsic test	Popular (Film)
STAR WARS[24] (ensemble)	MAYBE*	Degree of similarity at issue	Popular (Film)
Kaz[25]	NO	Included in scènes à faire	Prototype (Written summary, novel)
TRADING PLACES[26] (ensemble)	NO	Scènes à faire; similarities random, insignificant	Prototype (Screenplay)
E.T.[27]	NO	Scènes à faire; dissimilarities	Prototype (Live drama)
STAR WARS[28]	NO*	Substantial dissimilarities	Popular (Film)
A-Team[29]	NO	Insufficient delineation	Prototype (Script for TV pilot

*These decisions represent the same case. The Central District held that the characters, among other elements, were too dissimilar as a matter of law to sustain copyright infringement, but the Ninth Circuit reversed and remanded on the question.

Spade in terms of copyright protection in characters as such is the lack of delineation in the characters sought to be protected. Their "delineations" consisted of no more than a few lines of general description with a suggestion of the actor to assume each role.

Table 2
Formula for Predicting Copyright in Characters

```
Character = (Characterization + actions + reactions) =

            Expression

where

Characterization = (name and/or identity + physical

                    description + personality*)

                  (< Expression)

     *Personality = Character traits + patterns of thought

                   (< Expression)

Reactions = Responses to people + responses to situations

          (< Expression)
```

A PROPOSAL FOR RECONCILIATION OF COPYRIGHT DECISIONS

The foregoing discussion suggests that copyright protection in characters may not be so inconsistent as it first appears to be. Whether coextensive with the underlying work, subordinate to it, or somehow rising above it, characters are subjected to analysis based in evolving copyright law. The matter of similarity is crucial both to establishing the elements of copyright and to defending against infringement claims. Here the test is for development and delineation of character. A proposal for conducting that test follows. (See table 2.) The elements by which copyright is attached to a character are characterization, actions and reactions. Each element is comprised from the indicated components.

In order for character, whatever its relationship to the vehicle of presentation, to be protected all three elements of the proposed test must be covered in the character's development and delineation. Where all three elements are present in full, copyright can attach, subject to defenses other than scènes à faire. If any element or a substantial portion of any of the three is missing, the character is incomplete. That character is most likely a part of the scènes à faire.

Controversy will arise in that grey area along the continuum extending from idea, where at least one component is absent, and expression, where all three elements are present and complete. The simplest presentation is that in which the character and the work are coextensive. It occurs most often when cartoon characters or dolls are the subject matter of legal dispute.

Thus, in the case of Mutt and Jeff, the New York District finds actionable similarities in the names, physical appearance, costumes, and language of the properties. In this simple presentation, all three elements are obviously covered. Similarly, the cartoon Superman and his cartoon counterpart are actionably close where their physical appearance and costumes and their powers and feats are nearly identical. In more complex media, the relatively simplistic Francis and Amos and Andy still fulfill all three elements.

The test becomes far more significant to analysis where characters are subordinate to the work. Here infringement of the whole may encompass infringement of them, or their taking may assist in determining whether infringement exists. In either case, where the characters stand on the proposed continuum from idea to expression will ultimately be determinative. Assuming sufficient attention to characters in each precedent opinion, they can be placed along the continuum and the case law thereby reconciled.

If the characters at issue are merely scènes à faire, so intensive an analysis is unnecessary. By definition, such a case will not turn on similarity. But the test will be in point in determining the similarity needed for a prima facie case and for proceeding through the defenses, notably including parody.

Thus, Superman is not infringed by the Greatest American Hero, because their similar powers are handled differently because of differences in ability. Their respective actions and reactions to people and situations are quite different. Their personalities are totally dissimilar although both are proponents of truth, justice, and the American way.

McDonald's characters did, however, infringe on H. R. Pufnstuf and company. The unique appearance, developed personalities, and particular interactions of the latter had been assumed by the former.

The people and beings of *Battlestar Galactica* and their colleagues of *Star Wars* may or may not be actionably similar. Only by examining them in the course of trial can they be placed along the continuum. One court focused on dissimilarities, which can be placed among the elements set forth in table 2; another saw the potential similarities. Use of the continuum could guide the end result and render future decisions more obviously consistent.

There has yet to be a case analyzing a character overtly held independent and separable from the underlying works. Nevertheless, those who have been subject to protection by copyright or in the nature of copyright have certainly fulfilled all the elements of the test. Among these are the redoubtable Sam Spade, Scarlett O'Hara, Rhett Butler, Hopalong Cassidy, and Tarzan of the Apes.

Characters who have been found unworthy of protection are lacking most of the components of the three elements. Among them are the prototypes for the A-Team and Regan of *The Exorcist*.

Regan is something of a mystery, because she would seem to place high on the continuum. But the Central District of California seems to be holding that the defenses of scènes à faire and dissimilarity defeat her rather than lack of delineation. Regan is unique in that she is held to rise above the underlying work. It is she who subordinates it. Yet she is treated more as coextensive than as either subordinate or superior.

IS THERE A GAP IN LEGAL RECOGNITION OF CHARACTERS AS INTELLECTUAL PROPERTIES?

Given existing case law, there is probably no need to amend the Copyright Act expressly to include characters among the affected properties. A reconciliation of the lines of cases is, however, in order. In both approaches discussed here, the problematic case of Sam Spade can be "placed" without special analysis beyond that directed to the precedent and to successors in the Ninth, Second, and other federal circuits.

In short, deserving characters are protected by copyright. In most cases that protection will be expressed through licensing agreements, which must be studiously drafted to ensure the intended distribution and retention of all attendant properties. Where copyright constitutes insufficient protection or ceases to exist by operation of law, trademark and unfair competition can supplement its protection of popular fictional characters. There is, then, neither true inconsistency nor any gap in legal recognition of popular fictional characters as intellectual properties.

NOTES

(The case citations herein are abbreviations, followed by the chapter [in brackets] in which the case is first discussed and the subject character [in parentheses]. For a complete citation or more detail please turn to the bibliography or the referenced chapter.)

1. Prouty v. NBC, D. Mass. 1939 [5] (Stella Dallas).
2. Stern v. U.S., E.D. La. 1958 [5] (Francis).
3. Wavelength Film v. Columbia Pictures, N.D. Ill. 1986 [3] (Starman).
4. MGM v. Showcase Atlanta, N.D. Ga. 1981 [3] (Scarlett O'Hara and ensemble).
5. Trust Co. Bank v. MGM/UA, N.D. Ga. 1984 [5] (Scarlett O'Hara and ensemble).
6. Detective Comics v. Bruns Publications, 2d Cir. 1940 [6] (Superman).
7. Warner Bros. v. ABC, 2d Cir. 1981 [6] (Superman).
8. Hill v. Whalen & Martell, S.D. N.Y. 1914 [5] (Mutt and Jeff).
9. Filmvideo v. Hastings, S.D. N.Y. 1981 [5] (Hopalong Cassidy).
10. Silverman v. CBS, S.D. N.Y. 1986 [5] (Amos and Andy).
11. *See, e.g.,* Superman, *supra* note 7.
12. Amos and Andy, *supra* note 10. For purposes of ensuing discussions, a portrait is little more than superficial physical appearance, only one component of the characterization element of character as copyright.
13. Mutt and Jeff, *supra* note 8.
14. Hopalong Cassidy, *supra* note 9.
15. Giangrasso v. CBS, E.D. N.Y. 1982 [5] (WKRP ensemble).
16. Zambito v. Paramount, C.D. N.Y. 1985 [3] (Indiana Jones and ensemble).

17. Ideal v. Kenner, S.D. N.Y. 1977 [8] (*Star Wars* ensemble).
18. Smith v. Weinstein, S.D. N.Y. 1984 [3] (*Stir Crazy* ensemble).
19. Burroughs v. MGM, S.D. N.Y. 1981 [7] (Tarzan).
20. Warner Bros. v. CBS, 9th Cir. 1954 [5] (Sam Spade).
21. Warner Bros. v. Film Ventures, C.D. Cal. 1975 [5] (Regan).
22. Krofft v. McDonald's, 9th Cir. 1977 [2] (H. R. Pufnstuf).
23. Universal Studios v. J.A.R., C.D. Cal. 1982 (E.T.).
24. Twentieth Century-Fox v. MCA, 9th Cir. 1983 [3] (Luke Skywalker and ensemble).
25. Miller v. CBS, C.D. Cal. 1980 [2] (Kaz).
26. Anderson v. Paramount, C.D. Cal. 1985 [3] (*Trading Places* ensemble).
27. Litchfield v. Spielberg, 9th Cir. 1984 [3] (E.T.).
28. Twentieth Century-Fox v. MCA, C.D. Cal. 1980 [3] (Luke Skywalker and ensemble).
29. Olson v. NBC, 9th Cir. 1988 [5] (A-Team).
30. Luke Skywalker, *supra* note 24.
31. The A-Team, *supra* note 29.

Select Bibliography

OF THE LAW

Cases

The United States Supreme Court

Champion Spark Plug v. Sanders, 331 U.S. 125, 67 S. Ct. 1136 (1947)
Coca Cola v. Koke Co., 254 U.S. 143, 41 S. Ct. 113 (1920)
Compco Corp. v. Day-Brite Lighting, 376 U.S. 234, 84 S. Ct. 779 (1964)
International News Service v. Associated Press, 248 U.S. 215, 39 S. Ct. 68 (1918)
Mazer v. Stein, 347 U.S. 201, 74 S. Ct. 460 (1954)
Prestonettes v. Coty, 264 U.S. 359, 44 S. Ct. 350 (1924)
Sears Roebuck & Co. v. Stiffel Co., 376 U.S. 225, 84 S. Ct. 784 (1964)

Federal Courts of the Second Circuit

Alexander v. Haley, 460 F. Supp. 40 (S.D. N.Y. 1978)
Arnstein v. Porter, 154 F.2d 464 (2d Cir. 1946)
Bartsch v. Metro-Goldwyn-Mayer, 391 F.2d 150 (2d Cir. 1968)
Bayer Co. v. United Drug Co., 272 F. 505 (S.D. N.Y. 1921)
Berlin v. E.C. Publications, 329 F.2d 541 (2d Cir. 1964)

Bi-Rite Enterprises v. Button Master, 217 U.S.P.Q. 910 (S.D. N.Y. 1983)

Blake Publishing Corp. v. O'Quinn Studios, 202 U.S.P.Q. 848 (S.D. N.Y. 1979)

Burroughs v. Metro-Goldwyn-Mayer, 210 U.S.P.Q. 579 (S.D. N.Y. 1980)

Burroughs v. Metro-Goldwyn-Mayer, 215 U.S.P.Q. 37 (S.D. N.Y. 1981)

Burroughs v. Metro-Goldwyn-Mayer, 683 F.2d 610 (2d Cir. 1982)

Consumers Union of U.S. v. General Signal Corp., 724 F.2d 1044 (2d Cir. 1983)

Dallas Cowboys Cheerleaders v. Pussycat Cinema, 467 F. Supp. 366 (S.D. N.Y. 1979)

Davis v. United Artists, 547 F. Supp. 722 (S.D. N.Y. 1982)

DC Comics v. Filmation Associates, 486 F. Supp 1273 (S.D. N.Y. 1980)

DC Comics v. Powers, 201 U.S.P.Q. 99 (S.D. N.Y. 1978)

DC Comics v. Reel Fantasy, 217 U.S.P.Q. 307 (2d Cir. 1982)

Detective Comics v. Bruns Publications, 111 F 2d 432 (2d Cir. 1940)

Detective Comics v. Fawcett Publications, 64 U.S.P.Q. 594 (S.D. N.Y. 1944)

DuPont Cellophane Co. v. Waxed Products Co., 85 F.2d 75 (2d Cir. 1936)

Durham Industries v. Tomy Corp., 630 F.2d 905 (2d Cir. 1980)

Factors, Etc. v. Pro Arts, 652 F.2d 278 (2d Cir. 1981)

Feathercombs v. Solo Products Corporation, 306 F.2d 251 (2d Cir. 1962)

Filmvideo Releasing Corp. v. Hastings, 426 F. Supp. 690, 509 F. Supp. 60 (S.D. N.Y. 1981)

Filmways Pictures v. Marks Polarized Corp., 320 U.S.P.Q. 870 (S.D. N.Y. 1982)

Giangrasso v. CBS, 215 U.S.P.Q. 219 (E.D. N.Y. 1982)

Goodis v. United Artists Television, 425 F.2d 397 (2d Cir. 1970)

Groucho Marx Productions v. Day and Night Co., 689 F.2d 317 (2d Cir. 1982)

Haelen Laboratories v. Topps Chewing Gum, 202 F.2d 866 (2d Cir. 1953)

Harper & Row Publishers v. Nation Enterprises, 220 U.S.P.Q. 210 (S.D. N.Y. 1983)

Hill v. Whalen & Martell, 220 F. 359 (S.D. N.Y. 1914)

Hoehling v. Universal City Studios, 618 F.2d 972 (2d Cir. 1980)

Home Box Office v. Showtime/The Movie Channel, 665 F. Supp. 1079 (S.D. N.Y. 1987)

Ideal Toy Corp. v. Kenner Products Div., 197 U.S.P.Q. 738 (S.D. N.Y. 1977)

MacDonald v. Du Maurier, 144 F.2d 696 (2d Cir. 1944)
Mattel v. Azrack-Hamway International, 221 U.S.P.Q. 302 (2d Cir. 1983)
Mego Corp. v. Mattel, 203 U.S.P.Q. 377 (S.D. N.Y. 1978)
Midway Mfg. Co. v. Bandai-America, 216 U.S.P.Q. 812 (S.D. N.Y. 1982)
National Comics Publications v. Fawcett Publications, 191 F. 2d 594 (2d Cir. 1951)
Orion Pictures Co. v. Dell Pub. Co., 471 F. Supp. 392 (S.D. N.Y. 1979)
Paramount Pictures v. Rubinowitz, 217 U.S.P.Q. 48 (E.D. N.Y. 1981)
Paramount Pictures v. Worldwide Entertainment, 195 U.S.P.Q. 539 (S.D. N.Y. 1977)
Reyher v. Children's Television Workshop, 533 F.2d 87 (2d Cir. 1976)
G. Ricordo & Co. v. Paramount Pictures, 189 F.2d 469 (2d Cir. 1951)
Rossner v. CBS, 612 F. Supp. 334 (S.D. N.Y. 1985)
Sheldon v. Metro-Goldwyn-Mayer Pictures Corporation, 81 F.2d 49 (2d Cir. 1936)
Shipman v. R.K.O. Radio Pictures, 100 F.2d 533 (2d Cir. 1938)
Siegel v. National Periodical Publications, 508 F.2d 909 (2d Cir. 1974)
Silverman v. CBS, 632 F. Supp. 1344 (S.D. N.Y. 1986)
Smith v. Little, Brown & Company, 360 F.2d 928 (2d Cir. 1966)
Smith v. Weinstein, 578 F. Supp. 1297 (S.D. N.Y. 1984)
Spring Mills v. Ultracashmere House, 215 U.S.P.Q. 1057 (S.D. N.Y. 1982)
Tetley v. Topps Chewing Gum, 556 F. Supp. 785 (E.D. N.Y. 1983)
Universal City Studios v. Nintendo Co., 578 F. Supp. 911 (S.D. N.Y. 1983)
Warner Bros. v. American Broadcasting Companies, 654 F.2d 204 (2d Cir. 1981)
Warner Bros. v. American Broadcasting Cos., 215 U.S.P.Q. 690 (S.D. N.Y. 1982)
West v. Hatch, 49 F. Supp. 307 (S.D. N.Y. 1943)
Wiren v. Shubert Theatre Corporation, 5 F. Supp. 358 (S.D. N.Y. 1933)
Wyatt Earp Enterprises v. Sackman, 116 U.S.P.Q. 122 (S.D. N.Y. 1958)
Zambito v. Paramount Pictures Corp., 613 F. Supp. 1107 (C.D. N.Y. 1985)

Federal Courts of the Ninth Circuit

Anderson v. Paramount Pictures Corp., 617 F. Supp. (C.D. Cal. 1985)
Anti-Monopoly Inc. v. General Mills Fun Group, 684 F.2d 1316 (9th Cir. 1982)

Axelbank v. Rony, 277 F.2d 314 (9th Cir. 1960)
Berkic v. Crichton, 761 F.2d 1289 (9th Cir. 1985)
Bradbury v. Columbia Broadcasting System, 287 F.2d 478 (9th Cir. 1961)
Cher v. Forum International, 217 U.S.P.Q. 407 (9th Cir. 1982)
Columbia Pictures Corp. v. National Broadcasting Co., 137 F. Supp. 348 (S.D. Cal. 1955)
Columbia Pictures Industries v. Embassy Pictures, 218 U.S.P.Q. 497 (C.D. Cal. 1982)
Edgar Rice Burroughs v. Manns Theatres, 195 U.S.P.Q. 159 (C.D. Cal. 1976)
Jones v. Republic Productions, 46 U.S.P.Q. 175 (9th Cir. 1940)
Litchfield v. Spielberg, 736 F.2d 1352 (9th Cir. 1984)
Loew's Incorporated v. Columbia Broadcasting System, 131 F. Supp. 165 (S.D. Cal. 1955)
Miller v. Columbia Broadcasting System, 209 U.S.P.Q. 502 (C.D. Cal. 1980)
Olson v. National Broadcasting Co., 855 F.2d 1446 (9th Cir. 1988)
Russell v. Price, 612 F.2d 1123 (9th Cir. 1979)
Sid & Marty Krofft Television v. McDonald's Corp., 562 F.2d (9th Cir. 1977)
Sinatra v. Goodyear Tire & Rubber, 435 F.2d 711 (9th Cir. 1970)
Triangle Publications v. Knight-Ridder Newspapers, 626 F.2d 1171 (C.D. Cal. 1982)
Twentieth Century-Fox Film Corp. v. MCA, 209 U.S.P.Q. 200 (C.D. Cal. 1980)
Twentieth Century-Fox Film Corp. v. MCA, 715 F.2d 1327 (9th Cir. 1983)
Universal City Studios v. Film Ventures Intern., 214 U.S.P.Q. 865 (C.D. Cal. 1982)
Universal Studios v. J.A.R. Sales, 216 U.S.P.Q. 679 (C.D. Cal. 1982)
Walt Disney Productions v. Air Pirates, 581 F.2d 751 (9th Cir. 1978)
Walt Disney Productions v. Kusan, 204 U.S.P.Q. 284 (C.D. Cal. 1979)
Warner Bros. v. Film Ventures International, 403 F. Supp. 522 (C.D. Cal. 1975)
Warner Bros. Pictures v. Columbia Broadcasting System, 216 F. 2d 945 (9th Cir. 1954)

Other Federal Courts

Atari v. North American, Etc., 672 F.2d 607 (7th Cir. 1982)
Carson v. Here's Johnny Portable Toilets, 698 F.2d 831 (6th Cir. 1983)

Columbia Broadcasting System v. DeCosta, 377 F.2d 315 (1st Cir. 1967)
Conan Properties v. Conans Pizza, 752 F.2d 145 (5th Cir. 1985)
DeCosta v. Columbia Broadcasting System, 520 F.2d 499 (1st Cir. 1975)
Dr. Pepper Co. v. Sambo's Restaurants, 517 F. Supp. 1202 (N.D. Tex. 1981)
Franklin Mint Corp. v. Nat. Wildlife Art Exchg., 575 F.2d 62 (3d Cir. 1978)
Funkhouser v. Loew's Inc., 208 F.2d 185 (8th Cir. 1953)
Lone Ranger v. Cox, 50 U.S.P.Q. 577 (W.D. SC. 1941)
Lone Ranger v. Cox, 52 U.S.P.Q. 146 (4th Cir. 1942)
Lone Ranger v. Curry, 78 U.S.P.Q. 244 (M.D. Pa. 1948)
Metro-Goldwyn-Mayer v. Showcase Atlanta Co-op Prod., 479 F. Supp. 351 (N.D. Ga. 1981)
Miller v. Universal City Studios, 650 F.2d 1365 (5th Cir. 1981)
The Nestle Company v. Chester's Market, 219 U.S.P.Q. 298 (D. Conn. 1983)
O'Neill v. Dell Publishing Co., 630 F.2d 683 (1st Cir. 1980)
In re Polar Music International, 221 U.S.P.Q. 315 (Fed. Cir. 1983)
Prouty v. National Broadcasting Co., 26 F. Supp. 265 (D. Mass. 1939)
Selchow & Righter Co. v. Decipher, 598 F. Supp. 1489 (E.D. Va. 1984)
Selchow & Righter Co. v. Goldex Corp., 612 F. Supp. 19 (S.D. Fla. 1985)
Stern v. United States, 164 F. Supp. 847 (E.D. La. 1958)
Trust Co. Bank v. MGM/Ua Entertainment, 593 F. Supp. 580 (N.D. GA. 1984)
Universal City Studios v. Montgomery Ward & Co., 207 U.S.P.Q. 852 (N.D. Ill. 1980)
Universal Studios v. Kamar Industries, 217 U.S.P.Q. 1163 (S.D. Tex. 1982)
Wavelength Film v. Columbia Pictures, 631 F. Supp. 305 (N.D. Ill. 1986)

State Courts

American Broadcasting Co. v. Button World Mfg., 151 U.S.P.Q. 361 (N.Y. Sup. Ct. 1966)
Burroughs v. Metro-Goldwyn-Mayer, 130 U.S.P.Q. 245 (Cal. Super. Ct. 1961)
Fenton McHugh Productions v. WGN Continental Productions, 216 U.S.P.Q. 173 (Ill. App. 1982)

Guglielmi v. Spelling-Goldberg Productions, 205 U.S.P.Q. 1116 (Cal. Sup. Ct. 1979)
Lugosi v. Universal Pictures, 205 U.S.P.Q. 1090 (Cal. Sup. Ct. 1979)
Mann v. Columbia Pictures, 217 U.S.P.Q. 468 (Cal. App. 1982)
Martin Luther King, Jr. Center v. Amer. Heritage Products, 216 U.S.P.Q. 711 (Ga. Sup. Ct. 1982)
Weitzenkorn v. Lesser, 97 U.S.P.Q. 545 (Cal. Sup. Ct. 1953)

Commentary

Battersby and Grimes. *Protecting Merchandising Properties under Copyright Law, in* 1985 ENTERTAINMENT, PUBLISHING AND THE ARTS HANDBOOK.

Berman and Boxer. *Copyright Infringement of Audiovisual Works and Characters,* 52 CAL. L. REV. 315 (1979).

Chafee. *Reflections on the Law of Copyright: I,* 45 COLUM. L. REV. 503 (1945).

Diamond. *Properly Used, Trademarks Are Forever,* 68 A.B.A. J. 1575 (1982).

———. *The Public Interest and the Trademark System,* 62 J. PAT. OFF. SOC'Y 528 (1980).

Ginsberg. *Transfer of the Right of Publicity: Dracula's Progeny and Privacy's Stepchild,* 25 COPYRIGHT L. SYMP. (ASCAP) 1 (1980).

Marks. *Legal Rights and Fictional Characters,* 25 COPYRIGHT L. SYMP. (ASCAP) 35 (1980).

Phillips. *A Haystack in a Hurricane: A Divergent Case Law on the Right of Publicity and the Copyright Act of 1976,* 63 J. PAT. OFF. SOC'Y 296 (1981).

The Protection Afforded Literary and Cartoon Characters through Trademark, Unfair Competition, and Copyright, 68 HARV. L. REV. 349 (1954).

Rader. *The "Right of Publicity"—A New Dimension,* 61 J. PAT. OFF. SOC'Y 296 (1979).

Rohde. *Dracula, Still Undead (Unresolved Right-of-Publicity Questions Are Sure to Haunt the Courts), in* 1985. ENTERTAINMENT, PUBLISHING AND THE ARTS HANDBOOK.

Saidman. *Copyrights: Novelty or Originality?* 55 J. PAT. OFF. SOC'Y 314 (1973).

Wilson. *Visual Arts & the Law, in* LAW AND THE ARTS/ART AND THE LAW (T. HORWITZ ed. 1979).

Yankwich. *Originality in the Law of Intellectual Property (Its Meaning from a Legal and Literary Standpoint),* 11 F.R.D. 457 (1952).

Books and Treatises

EPSTEIN, M. MODERN INTELLECTUAL PROPERTY (1984).
NIMMER, M., AND NIMMER, D. NIMMER ON COPYRIGHT (1988).
STRONG, W. THE COPYRIGHT BOOK/A PRACTICAL GUIDE (2d ed. 1984).

OF THE RELATED SUBSTANCE

Primary Sources

BURROUGHS, E. TARZAN OF THE APES (1914), THE RETURN OF TARZAN (1915), THE BEASTS OF TARZAN (1916), TARZAN AND THE JEWELS OF OPAR (1918), JUNGLE TALES OF TARZAN (1919), TARZAN THE UNTAMED (1920), TARZAN THE TERRIBLE (1921), TARZAN AND THE CITY OF GOLD (1938).
DUDLEY, E., AND NOVAK, M., eds. THE WILD MAN WITHIN (1972).
Itard, *The Wild Boy of Aveyron* (1799–1806), *in* L. MALSON, WOLF CHILDREN AND THE PROBLEM OF HUMAN NATURE (1972).
KIPLING, R. THE JUNGLE BOOKS (1961 ed.).
MALSON, L. WOLF CHILDREN AND THE PROBLEM OF HUMAN NATURE (1972).
TRUFFAUT, F., AND GRUAULT, J. THE WILD CHILD (trans. Lewin and Lemery 1973).

Background in the Humanities and Popular Culture

ANONYMOUS. SUPERMAN/FROM THE THIRTIES TO THE SEVENTIES (1971).
ESSOE, G. TARZAN OF THE MOVIES (1968).
HOLTSMARK, E. TARZAN AND TRADITION/CLASSICAL MYTH IN POPULAR LITERATURE (1981).
LICHTENBERG, J., MARSHAK, S., AND WINSTON, J. STAR TREK LIVES! (1975).
LUPOFF, R. EDGAR RICE BURROUGHS: MASTER OF ADVENTURE (1965).
MUNN, M. GREAT FILM EPICS/THE STORIES BEHIND THE SCENES (1982).
PETROU, D. THE MAKING OF SUPERMAN, THE MOVIE (1978).
PORGES, I. EDGAR RICE BURROUGHS/THE MAN WHO CREATED TARZAN (1975).
LORD RAGLAN. THE HERO/A STUDY IN TRADITION, MYTH AND DRAMA (1956, 1975 ed.).

ROTHEL, D. WHO WAS THAT MASKED MAN?/THE STORY OF THE LONE RANGER™ (rev. ed. 1981).

WHITFIELD, S., AND RODDENBERRY, G. THE MAKING OF STAR TREK (1968).

Index

About the Author

DOROTHY J. HOWELL, currently an adjunct visiting professor at Vermont Law School and a visiting professor at Franklin Pierce Law School, is a freelance counsel whose areas of special interest include intellectual property and environmental law. The subject of legal protection for fictional characters is a specialty of Professor Howell's, as she is the author of several novels as well as scholarly materials for a variety of professional audiences.

www.ingramcontent.com/pod-product-compliance
Ingram Content Group UK Ltd.
Pitfield, Milton Keynes, MK11 3LW, UK
UKHW020207290926
15470UKWH00001B/39

9 780899 305066